CONVERSATIONS
WITH
GHOSTS

CONVERSATIONS
WITH
GHOSTS

BY

To Joolo
with best wishes

Alex Tanous, D.D.

with

Callum E. Cooper
(Editor & Contributor)

www.whitecrowbooks.com

Conversations with Ghosts

Published and printed in the United States of America
and the United Kingdom by White Crow Books; an
imprint of White Crow Productions Ltd.

White Crow Books
at 3 Merrow Grange, Horseshoe Lane East,
Guildford, GU1 2QW, United Kingdom
e-mail: info@whitecrowbooks.com.

Cover Designed by Butterflyeffect
Interior design by Velin@Perseus-Design.com

Paperback ISBN 978-1-908733-55-9
eBook   ISBN 978-1-908733-56-6

Non Fiction / Body, Mind & Spirit / Parapsychology

Published by White Crow Books
www.whitecrowbooks.com

ACKNOWLEDGEMENTS

I extend my thanks to several people for helping the construction of this new insight into the work of the late Dr Alex Tanous. Thanks to Alice Kelley (Secretary of the Alex Tanous Foundation), for sifting through the material related to Alex and his investigations of hauntings, and for her encouragement of the project. Thanks also go to Loyd Auerbach for allowing me to use material from his own publications regarding Alex, and for sharing his thoughts and experiences on various issues. I'm grateful to Jennifer Allen for her memories of Alex and his investigation of ghosts and hauntings. Thank you for sharing the past, so that we might learn more about the present – and the future.

With additional thanks to Tony Tricker and David Ellis for their editorial suggestions on earlier drafts of this book.

The construction of this short yet insightful book would not have been made possible without the support and assistance of:

The Alex Tanous Foundation for Scientific Research
(Portland, Maine, USA)

&

The Society for Psychical Research's Survival Committee
(London, UK)

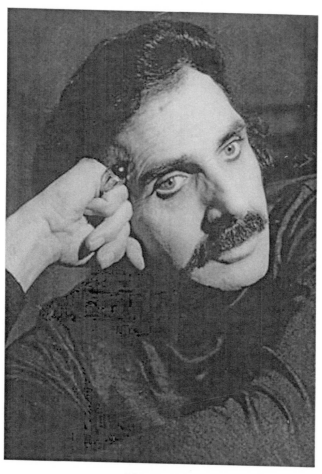

Alex Tanous

CONTENTS

INTRODUCTION

Conversations with Ghosts is a collection of investigation accounts written by the late Dr Alex Tanous. These investigations covered a variety of haunting-type phenomena, including apparitions, objects purportedly moving on their own (poltergeist phenomenon) and other strange sights and sounds. Dr Tanous left behind a wealth of writings, and *Conversations with Ghosts* was one of them. However, it was an unpublished manuscript consisting of only three chapters.

It was intended to be completed as a collection of case reports by Dr Tanous and Dr Karlis Osis of the American Society for Psychical Research. (The Society was founded in 1884, by the famous psychologist and philosopher William James, two years after the establishment of the British SPR in 1882 by several noted Cambridge scholars. The remit of both Societies was, and still is, to investigate paranormal phenomena in a serious and scientific manner, without prejudice). However, Dr Tanous never finished this insightful and valuable addition to parapsychological literature. Therefore, I felt it was time for the book to be completed by bringing together a number of Dr Tanous' unpublished notes and personal thoughts on hauntings and apparitions, to fill in the missing gaps in the manuscript.

For many parapsychologists, and related researchers, Dr Tanous is perhaps a rather unique individual who may have slipped under the radar, particularly where British researchers are concerned. Though he had travelled worldwide, his fame was predominantly in the United States of America.

Alexander Tanous was born on 26 November, 1926, in Van Buren, Maine. He was the eldest of several siblings in the family. Before he was born, his father was counselled by Kahlil Gibran, the famous Lebanese writer and author of *The Prophet* (Gibran, 1923). The prediction from Gibran to Tanous' father was: "You will have a son, a man of exceptional gifts, of great abilities – but also a man of great sorrows." This prediction came true. From a young age of just a few years, Tanous foresaw the deaths of family members and close friends, made predictions about world events, knew what people were doing some distance away, and also had several imaginary childhood friends. The latter events are what Dr Tanous believed to be a common experience for many children, the ability to see and interact with ghosts. His own 'imaginary' friends were confirmed by his family to be deceased friends and relatives when he described who they were, what they looked like, and things they said.

All of these remarkable experiences throughout his life, and more, were discussed in his autobiography entitled *Beyond Coincidence*, compiled with the help of Harvey Ardman (Tanous, with Ardman, 1976). His second book explored his interest in the natural, innocent experiences and abilities of children which appear to suggest psychic potentials present in their everyday behaviour, which often goes unnoticed. This book was compiled as an academic study, entitled *Is Your Child Psychic?*, co-authored by Katherine Fair Donnelly (Tanous & Donnelly, 1979).

Turning to education, Dr Tanous gained an impressive variety of qualifications, including an undergraduate degree in theology, three masters degrees in philosophy (Boston College), theology (Fordham University), and education and counselling (University of Maine at Portland, which later became the University of Southern Maine in 1978). He also completed doctoral research and gained a doctorate in divinity (D.D., theology) from the College of Divine Metaphysics (Indiana). Additionally, he qualified as a school psychologist and a marriage counsellor. His education and teaching life suffered from time to time because of his psychic abilities, the display of which in public his teachers and priests often frowned upon, even though there were some who were fairly supportive of psychic phenomena.

Throughout his teaching life, he had been given numerous positions as a lecturer in theology and philosophy, but throughout the most prominent part of his career he gave lectures on parapsychology, healing, and dreams, at the University of Southern Maine. This was the first course on parapsychology to be offered 'with credit'. The course itself was not hidden under the title of psychology, philosophy, or theology – as many academic institutions do to hide from the potential criticism which can come with offering courses on the paranormal – it was simply listed as a class in parapsychology, and it brought in thousands of students.

Many of his dream-classes were recorded and became part of his third and final published book, entitled *Dreams, Symbols and Psychic Power*, which was compiled and completed with the help of Timothy Gray (Tanous & Gray, 1990). Many have found this book an extremely useful guide to dream interpretation, helping make sense of dreams and their symbolic meaning (e.g., dreaming of flying, teeth falling out, interacting with the dead, and so on).

When reading through the vast amount of literature on psychical research and parapsychology, references to Dr Tanous and accounts of his psychic abilities crop up in a variety of places, which give an insight into what he was really like and what people thought of him beyond his own accounts (Tanous, with Ardman, 1976). Perhaps his most well-known scientifically researched feats would be the investigation of his out-of-body experiences (OBEs).

Greenhouse (1974) discussed several instances of Dr Tanous' out-of-body ability, in his book entitled *The Astral Journey*. Not only was Dr Tanous impressed, and at the same time confused, by these experiences, he had also heard reports from several dying friends that they had experienced an out-of-body state, as though they were entering another realm of existence. These included feelings and sensations of drifting, flying above one's own body, looking down, or travelling to distant locations and observing what people were doing. Intrigued by this, he spent several years working in a hospital, for the express purpose of studying terminally ill patients. This was done in an attempt to learn more about the possibility of the survival of the mind beyond death. Frequently, dying patients saw apparitions of deceased friends and family.

It was at this point in time, that Dr Tanous was inevitably going to find common ground with Dr Karlis Osis, who had co-written a book with Prof Erlendur Haraldsson on the experiences of the dying (Osis & Haraldsson, 1977). Researching survival was their key interest, and experimental tests of the OBE was one such potential way of demonstrating externalised conscious awareness – the mind being active outside the body.

Throughout the 1970s and early 1980s, Dr Tanous was one of the main experimental subjects for the American Society for Psychical Research, which is where he became acquainted with Dr Osis. In the main, he was investigated for his claim of out-of-body capabilities, though numerous other studies regarding Dr Tanous were also explored. In total, he spent around twenty years in association with the ASPR. Dr Osis even published one of his most extensive studies on OBEs with Dr Tanous as the sole participant (Osis & McCormick, 1980). The study produced remarkable results. Its aim was not only to see if Dr Tanous could project his mind beyond the body and view target images at a distance, but also to measure whatever was supposedly leaving the body during this process (i.e., human consciousness, the mind, the spirit, etc.).

Not only did Dr Tanous produce, on average, a ninety per cent hit rate through perceiving a target image four rooms away – being produced in an optical illusion box – but strain-gauges were also *active* in front of the box during periods of the *higher* clustered hit rates. This suggested that some form of 'presence' was affecting the strain-gauge, and it was left open to scientific debate as to what could have caused this result (Rogo, 1986; Cooper, 2013). That is, if it wasn't Dr Tanous' own astral travelling mind being detected, which was also responsible for him obtaining high hit rates (correctly guessed targets).

When these OBE studies were conducted, a room was converted especially for Dr Tanous which allowed him to lie down on the floor on cushions and pillows, in almost complete darkness. He could communicate with Dr Osis, who was four rooms away, via an intercom system. The room allowed Dr Tanous to attempt a number of psychic abilities, including exploring haunted locations from the comfort of the laboratory (much like remote viewing). He could relax his arms and legs and essentially experience sensory deprivation. This allowed him to focus more clearly on any potential psychic impressions which came to him. In modern parapsychological studies, this technique – though a little more advanced – is known as the Ganzfeld (a technique developed from psychology into parapsychology most notably by the late Charles Honorton).

In one remarkable session of testing the OBE, Dr Tanous stated that it had suddenly gone dark, he couldn't see anything, he couldn't see the targets. He specifically said that the optical illusion box – in which the targets were housed and generated – had gone dark. The experimenters could not make sense of his complaint; 'was it an excuse, or perhaps a failure of his psychic abilities?' they may have thought. On the contrary. The experimenters examined the box and found that the bulb inside the box illuminating the images had burnt out. "Needless to say, Dr Tanous could have had no normal way of knowing that something was wrong with the light," Scott Rogo stated (1987, p.162).

Other psychic abilities, which he was reported to display, include the seldom mentioned phenomenon of 'light projection'. In June 1974, the New Horizons Research Foundation – incorporating transactions of the Toronto Society for Psychical Research – held a conference on the subject of 'Psychokinesis and Related Phenomena'. Drs Osis and Tanous attended this conference, both giving presentations and demonstrations. Dr Tanous presented two talks, one on OBEs (Tanous, 1975a) and the second on 'Experiences with Light' (Tanous, 1975b). In the latter presentation, he discussed several instances in which he allegedly projected light, and images, from his eyes on to walls, for all those present to witness. In one such case, Dr Tanous visited the Myers family in Manchester, New Hampshire. After discussing paranormal phenomena over dinner, Dr Tanous then told the family he would project an image on to the wall for all of the family to see. Everyone reported seeing the image of a man, a clear outline of a head and shoulders, something they insisted was not a mere shadow, but an illuminated area, which progressed across the wall. They blinked, rubbed their eyes, but the image remained. Everyone present swore an affidavit which was given to Dr Osis, who then got the statement confirmed on audio-tape.

Later, Dr Tanous was tested at the Dream Laboratory in the Maimonides Medical Center. He was required to look at an image and then produce it as a pattern of light on the wall. Dr Alan Vaughan and Charles Honorton, as the researchers (and witnesses to the event), said they saw something being projected on the wall in the darkened room, but were not sure whether the images were objective or just telepathic projections from Dr Tanous' mind to theirs (or even pure suggestion). Nevertheless, the most remarkable of these experiences with light was discussed by Timothy Gray in the preface to Dr Tanous' third book. Gray wrote about an event in which his agent met Dr Tanous for the first time at the home of a mutual friend. At one point during the evening, Tanous held out his arm, and allegedly focused his energy so intensely that a ball of light materialised in the palm of his hand. All the witnesses present saw this ball of light, apart from Mr Gray's agent. However, she thought that her poor vision might have been to blame. The next morning, she awoke with perfect vision, thinking she'd left her contact lenses in overnight. She realised she hadn't, and after five minutes or so her vision declined. Dr Tanous later told her that he had visited her that morning in the astral body. She believed her spontaneous perfect vision was in some way related to Tanous and his abilities (see Tanous & Gray, 1990, pp. xiii-xiv).

In an interview with *The Greenwich Review* (Saxton, 1984), Dr Tanous stated that "Parapsychology is the search for immortality" (p. 21). Certainly, since the beginnings of psychical research, the initial scientific exploration had been to investigate whether the mind is capable of surviving the death of the body in some form – or not. As parapsychology developed in the university setting from the 1930s onwards, scientific testing for psychic phenomena became its main priority. There are still various scientists and researchers involved with survival research, and it was certainly the key research interest of Dr Tanous. For example, the research conducted with Dr Osis on Dr Tanous' out-of-body abilities were one issue which addressed the suggestion of the mind being able to operate outside the body. This form of survival research was top priority for the Tanous/Osis team. Second priority went to the investigations of haunting phenomena. Both sets of studies could potentially provide evidence for the survival of consciousness beyond the body, or even beyond death.

There is not a great deal of information in any one place on Dr Tanous regarding ghosts and hauntings, though there are numerous brief mentions in the available literature. Therefore, up until now, many have not been aware of the interest Dr Tanous had in ghosts, poltergeists, and hauntings. Auerbach (1986) gives brief mention to the haunting investigations of Drs Tanous and Osis, and even interviewed Dr Tanous on these issues (see Appendix 1). He also discussed some seldom-mentioned cases of Dr Tanous' out-of-body abilities in which people witnessed his bilocation (see Auerbach, 1986, p.43). This is where people appear to be in two places at once, which we could also describe as an apparition of the living. On several occasions, Dr Tanous was reported and verified to be in one place, while someone in another state or even country reported to have been with him having a lengthy conversation. In one such case, Dr Tanous was in New York resting in a hotel, while a friend of his in Canada reported that he heard a knock at the door late one evening and had to get out of bed to answer it. Discovering it was Alex at the door, he invited him in and they sat down for a while, drank tea and had a friendly conversation. The man's wife stayed in bed upstairs but heard the conversation. When Alex left, his friend waited for the sound of a car driving away, but heard nothing. He went back to the front-door to see if Alex was having car trouble due to the snowy weather. When he peered out the door, there was no sign of a car, or Alex, or any footprints in the snow leading away from the house. Dr Tanous later noted that his friend wrote down this strange experience and mailed it to him, and when Dr Tanous awoke that night at 3 a.m. in New York he too wrote down his *dream* of having visited his friend in Canada. Dr Osis was shown the two accounts and confirmed that the time at which the events took place did indeed match. It was these kinds of experiences suggesting that Dr Tanous could astral project and be 'seen' in the astral body, which led to serious experimental research on the matter at the ASPR.

Aside from Dr Tanous being able to project his own apparition, which he and several researchers considered to be important evidence for survival research, apparitions of the dead were equally of interest to Dr Tanous and his research. Myers (1986) published accounts of a collection of haunted sites in America that were on record as having been investigated by noted and respected researchers and psychics. This included several locations which are scarcely known to have been investigated by Dr Tanous. Such locations include Beckett's Castle and a handful of personal homes, as well as farmhouses and flats in and around Maine and New York. One particularly famous location that Dr Tanous investigated was the home of the Lutz family, the well-known Amityville case which was grossly exaggerated by the media (see Appendix 2).

On the subject of hauntings, in the book *Beyond Coincidence*, Dr Tanous gives a brief insight into his experiences of ghosts and hauntings. However, this chronicles stories of only a few of the haunted locations he visited and investigated, and the odd theory here and there as to what ghosts may be, if indeed they are an objective thing beyond hallucinations created through suggestion, dreams and other possibilities. Although Dr Tanous' background was in theology, he was sceptical of the paranormal and claims of survival beyond death, and was open to and respectful of other people's views and religious beliefs (such as those who wished to conduct exorcisms). He stated:

I have, on several occasions, made contact with ghosts and spirits. I am not a medium – at least not a

classic medium, the sort who holds séances, goes into
trances, etc. As far as spiritualism, mysticism, and the
occult are concerned, I'm a sceptic. I feel the same
way about possession by spirits and exorcisms.

(TANOUS, WITH ARDMAN, 1976, P. 149)

Such statements by Tanous are accompanied by others such as: "More harm can be done than good if you
get just anybody to investigate your house for ghosts."
He frequently made such statements in newspaper ar-
ticles, and urged people to contact the ASPR if they had
any strange experiences in their homes. His concerns
were not only with the haunting, but with the family's
and witness's well-being in the presence of whatever
strange phenomena was encountered. Therefore, he felt
such issues should be approached by the right professionals in a scientific manner, while ensuring confi-
dentiality for those involved.

In this long-awaited fourth publication of Dr Tanous'
work and remarkable experiences, the readers are able
to get an insight into the step-by-step investigations
that Tanous carried out with Dr Osis and others. It
also explains how he interacted and communicated
with 'ghosts' and discusses, among other things, his
thoughts and theories on spirits of the dead and the
afterlife. All of this for over two decades has been left
as a partial manuscript and a few notes thankfully

saved by the Alex Tanous Foundation for Scientific Research (Portland, Maine). The Foundation itself was established at the request of Dr Tanous – he passed away in 1990, after a battle with cancer and subsequent heart failure.

I hope readers will appreciate what an interesting and sorely missed character Dr Alex Tanous was, not only as a psychic, but also uniquely, and contradictorily, as a parapsychologist too. Therefore, a lot of the statements within this book, about ghosts and their occurrence, must be understood as having come from Dr Tanous' personal views and experiences as a psychic. However, it must also be kept in mind that he was, equally, a skilled and well-qualified researcher, and had spent nearly two decades working closely with many well-accomplished scientists, most notably, Dr Karlis Osis.

I feel honoured in being given the opportunity to piece together this new addition to Dr Tanous' works, with the forever encouraging support of the Alex Tanous Foundation for Scientific Research. The writings and lectures that Dr Tanous left behind are an enlightening insight into human potential and the limits of consciousness, which now remain for people to learn from for generations to come.

Callum E. Cooper
University of Northampton
Centre for the Study of Anomalous
Psychological Processes

References

Auerbach, L. (1986). *ESP, Hauntings and Poltergeists: A Parapsychologist's Handbook*. New York: Warner Books.

Cooper, C. E. (2013). "Out of the body and into the lab: Defining Dr Alex Tanous' abilities". *Paranthropology: Journal of Anthropological Approaches to the Paranormal, 4* (1a), 76–79.

Gibran, K. (1923). *The Prophet*. New York: Alfred A. Knopf.

Greenhouse, H. B. (1974). *The Astral Journey*. New York: Doubleday.

Myers, A. (1986). *The Ghostly Register: A Guide to Haunted America*. New York: Dorset Press.

Osis, K., & Haraldsson, E. (1977). *At the Hour of Death*. New York: Avon.

Osis, K., & McCormick, D. (1980). "Kinetic effects at the ostensible location of an out-of-body projection during perceptual testing". *Journal of the American Society for Psychical Research*, 74 (3), 319–329.

Rogo, D. S. (1986). "Researching the out-of-body experience: The state of the art". In K. A. Rao (Ed.) *Case Studies in Parapsychology* (pp. 97–119). London: McFarland & Co.

Rogo, D. S. (1987). *Psychic Breakthroughs Today*. Northamptonshire: Aquarian Press.

Saxton, D. B. (1984). "Psychic Phenomena, ESP, and apparitions". *The Greenwich Review*, October Issue, 17–21.

Tanous, A. (1975a). "Out-of- body experiences". *New Horizons*, 1 (5), 231–232.

Tanous, A. (1975b). "Experiences with light". *New Horizons*, 1 (5), 246–247.

Tanous, A., with Ardman, H. (1976). *Beyond Coincidence: One Man's Experiences with Psychic Phenomena*. New York: Doubleday & Co.

Tanous, A., & Donnelly, K. F. (1979). *Is Your Child Psychic? A Guide for Creative Parents and Teachers.* New York: MacMillan.

Tanous, A., & Gray, T. (1990). *Dreams, Symbols, and Psychic Power.* New York: Bantam Books.

Conversations with Ghosts

1

GHOSTS AND THE
HUNTERS

For almost 20 years, in association with the American Society for Psychical Research (ASPR), Dr Karlis Osis and I investigated apparitions, hauntings, and out-of-body experiences (OBEs). Alongside assisting in psychic crime detection and government work, I also made a name for myself as one of the foremost ghost hunters in the country.

Apparitions are not, as is commonly believed, *all* more or less alike. They vary widely. Some are perceived as an unrecognizable mist, others are so lifelike they are almost, or often, mistaken for real people. Some behave as though they are re-enacting shadows of tragic events from the past, others act only in the here-and-now and relate directly to observers. At times, apparitions are seen by everyone present – even by cats, dogs, and other household pets. On other occasions, apparitions are an entirely private experience like extra-sensory perception (ESP), invisible to all but one person. There are apparitions who associate themselves with personal objects and apparitions who recur again and again in so-called haunted houses.

After years of experience, Dr Osis and I learned to rule out apparitions occurring around certain pre-existing conditions. We also steered away from psycho-kinetic-type phenomena (PK), where adolescents had typically been present, which we would more commonly refer to as poltergeist phenomenon. Often, as any Stephen King reader knows, adolescents will create their own PK fields and phenomena, albeit unconsciously, while conscious trickery might also take place. These types of cases were disregarded by us, as they are not representative of true manifestations.

I was reluctant to explore reported cases where emotional strain existed in the family or inhabitants of the house. Overwrought emotional states can contribute to the manifestation of phenomena with similar effects to those caused by adolescents, with regards to PK and/ or poltergeist activity.

At the ASPR, Dr Osis would take phone calls pertaining to hauntings or observed apparitions. He collected all the information which would determine whether or not the case warranted further investigation. At that point, the case was brought to my attention. If I felt any interest in the site, then Dr Osis and I would visit the house. On the first visit, family members were sent out of the house, after which I would walk through the rooms gathering psychic impressions, while interacting with Dr Osis. All of these conversations were recorded on tape. Dr Osis would question me in an attempt to clarify the reported phenomena and perhaps give tentative explanations and suggestions. After our discussions, the family were invited back into their home to answer questions which might have helped explain certain events.

When the family was reassembled, Dr Osis often broke the ice by asking, "Alex, will you tell them what you found? What do we have to reconcile here?"

The first visit by Dr Osis and myself would generally be followed by a second, which was often an extensive all-night vigil, during which we would watch and record the manifestations with various test instruments. Spontaneous paranormal phenomena are difficult to pin-point. Therefore, it becomes a difficult task to get various sensing devices (such as motion sensors, for example) in the right spot at the moment the activity occurs. Dr Osis' assistant, Donna McCormick, would place various sensory equipment all over the house to monitor environmental changes. Typically, an infra-red beam would be used to detect movement and motion in the area where there had been the most reports of

3

'ghostly traffic' (i.e., the witnessing of moving apparitions). Strain-gauges and thermostats were placed in
the most active rooms, and TV monitors and chart re-
corders were installed on stairway landings.

The chart recorder was tailor-made to help Dr Osis
record several of the physical events often associated
with apparitions. For instance, if an apparition was reported to walk up and down a stairway, the stairway
would be staked out with a recorder. The equipment
can record movements and vibrations via strain-gauge
sensors in any location under investigation, just as I
had been monitored in the ASPR using similar equipment during out-of-body experiments, in an attempt to
record evidence suggestive of my mind/consciousness
travelling outside of my body. Strain-gauge sensors detect small movements and register them permanently
on strips of paper on the chart recorder (note: this is
now done on computer in modern experiments). Con-
currently, Dr Osis could also tape any walking sounds
associated with the reported apparitions. This information was then analysed with specialized custom-
built equipment: the sound would be slowed down
to approximately one-fifth of its original speed so the
sound waves can be visually traced, then the various
frequency wavebands of the noise would be graphed
one by one onto the strip-chart recorder. In addition
to the sound equipment, extremely sensitive thermom-
eters would be used to register split-second changes in
even very slight drops in temperature.

After the data was compiled from the various sensory devices, as well as from my psychic impressions, the historical records – of a house, site, or persons represented in the haunting – were researched and added to the case study for the ASPR files.

Once all the information was gathered, I would begin to counsel the ghost(s). If the ghost wanted information passing on to a living friend or relative, I would see it done. If the dead needed to be reconciled in some way, then I would make sure both parties understood exactly what had happened during the event in question. If it was a case of injustice that must be rectified, I would see the situation was adjusted to the specifications of the ghost. Occasionally, with the help of an object previously owned by the deceased, I would solve the case over the telephone.

The majority of cases in the ASPR files are closed, but not all of them were easily solved. Sometimes I would have to go back and resume my work in a haunted location. When I was finished, if the ghost no longer disturbed the house or the site, the event which had caused the ghost or person discord within the house was then termed to be reconciled.

I, like many people, believe that ghosts exist because they must tell their story to someone who can set their lives and actions into balance. I agree, however, that it will always be a metaphysical question as to why ghosts appear. If, as some religions promise, existence after death is a happy and fulfilling experience in the vastness of eternity, why would an apparition choose to limit itself to our world? Is the entity progressing towards some sort of consciousness? Are apparitions simply imprinted energy fields rooted to a particularly charged intense emotional incident like the shadowed after-image of an atomic blast?

It is my belief that the entity is, in fact, moving forward in its own consciousness, but, at times has the ability to return for the sole purpose of 'balancing unsupportable events or human injustice in experiences where they lived'. At the appropriate time, the entity can create an apparition (or related phenomena: movements, bangs and raps, etc.) whose aim it is to restore the universe to harmony, including his or her own individuality within the wholeness of the universe. This can be done in any way the entity sees fit, because both the cause and concept of the injustice began with the entity itself. From there, I feel it is up to the overriding consciousness of the apparition to decide what it wants to do about a given situation and how it wishes to convey its cry for help and understanding. Sometimes, in begging for help, an entity will cause horrible things to happen (i.e., poltergeist activity directed at people).

A common cause of any appearance of an apparition is when another person tries to restore or change a setting or house by adding an extra wing to the building, dividers to a room, a wall to demarcate property – anything that represents physical change. In these instances the entity doesn't understand it is now in a different dimension

6

and resents the fact that its world is being altered in an attempt to suit the needs of other people.

Ghosts will often haunt a location where they feel an injustice has been done, in a frail attempt to balance the cosmos and restore harmony to the universe through the attempts of the living to intervene for them and the perceived 'cause'. Ghosts will also manifest if the situation of the living people in the house or site at all resembles the situation in which the ghost found itself before death. For example, ghosts who had mourned the death of children during life will often attach themselves to living children in the house. In other cases, if a promise has been broken, a ghost will manifest in order to remind the living that they have responsibilities to keep their promises, even to people who have long since died.

And there are cases in which a ghost will manifest out of a simple love of life. Sometime during the early 1980s, at a summer seminar held at a small college in New England (USA), I was showing another psychic around a lake on campus. Both of us saw a little girl playing with two dogs. As we watched, the little girl rushed into the bushes and came out moments later followed by only the larger dog. After asking around, we discovered that the small dog once belonged to a student. The dog had died but it came back to the lake because it loved to play.

Many people agree that personality survives death and that we all have certain sensitive and inexplicable powers which alert our subconscious to dangers, allowing us to collect information on a highly subconscious and non-rational level. I maintain that everyone has spontaneous psychic powers that come into operation as long as the external consciousness and the medium have an agreement that the entity can and will talk to the medium.

Let's take this a step further. If we can assume that there is a consciousness at the site of a disturbing incident, it can reveal itself in ways that are almost like slow-motion replays. In fact, I would describe my perception of these occurrences as almost like watching a movie of the incident itself. Following that, the entity steps in, and through what I describe as a one-on-one dialogue, it gives the means of reconciliation and settlement of balance to me. During this interaction, I'm not my everyday self. I often undergo a change of consciousness similar to that which I displayed during the out-of-body experiments conducted at the ASPR by Dr Osis.

Ghostly manifestations are not quite as random as they may appear. There are no truly evil ghosts; any unpleasant effects of the presence are only the results of an unhappy lingering energy resulting from the act of injustice or imbalance itself. This event does not influence the individuality of the entity. But it is their individuality and personal choices which result in the decisions made as to how to rectify any detachment from the binding echo of the event, in which it has found itself bonded.

In some cases, it is even possible for ghosts to be in two places at once. A ghost can appear to a dying relative, haunt a site, and be seen by a living person at the same time. However, this is not so strange when one considers the acceptance and documentation of OBEs in living human beings.

In answer to the original question as to why ghosts persist in this material world when there is a beautiful 'afterlife' awaiting them, the answer could be that ghosts are still Earthbound because the part of them that manifests on the Earthly plane is attempting to deal the best way they know how with urgent unfinished business. From investigating apparitions, strange appearances, and hauntings, it is my job to act as a 'ghost psychologist' and help the troubled entity to work out its problems on a one-to-one basis in the same way I would go about helping people suffering in everyday life. I've made it my job to find out why the apparitions appear, what they're unhappy about, and what they feel should be done to rectify the situation. Counselling, and conversations with the ghosts, can then proceed in order to help them make peace with the situation, which they seem unable to leave.

2

HOUSES WITH MULTIPLE MANIFESTATIONS

Houses with multiple layers of consciousness are perhaps the most difficult cases to solve. Very old places or sites often have events attached to them, that begin with one key parallel dramatic event which triggers the same type of recurring behaviour in subsequent inhabitants of the site, which can be called the spiralling effect. Spiralling effects occur when multiple manifestations converge on a site, drawing to the house people with similar character weaknesses as the original inhabitants who had begun the cycle with a specific psychic event to which they are eternally attached.

Cedar Rapids

The Cedar Rapids case is a good example of a house with multiple manifestations, in which several incidents relating to children had made the house sensitive to pre-schoolers.

One rainy afternoon in the autumn of 1980, Dr Osis received a call at the ASPR. In a relatively calm voice, a young woman named Mindy began to relate the occurrences which had recently disturbed her family. She, her husband, and their son lived in a beautiful old farm house hidden from the road behind a stand of maples. A well cared for lawn stretched all the way from the house down to the two-lane highway. It was a peaceful setting, an ideal dream house and a good place to raise children. But the former inhabitants of the house were far from happy.

For a year, Mindy and her husband had heard things in the house late at night, but never with any regularity. Most of the noises they managed to ignore. They liked their home and didn't mind the occasional light switches being turned on and off, objects moving around with no explanations, doors slamming, or even the sound of a woman weeping from the upstairs master bedroom. But when their five-year-old son, Stevie, started to have horrible nightmares about people fighting over a child, and telling his mother that a little boy had died in his room, Mindy started to worry.

Stevie's nightmares got worse and worse until finally he became terrified of sleeping at all. He complained of being shut up in a small dark room, although his room was really big and airy. At her wit's end, Mindy called the ASPR.

Dr Osis assured her that he, and I, would work on the case. At the time, I had several important speaking engagements which did not allow me to go to Cedar Rapids. The matter was discussed between us and we agreed to investigate the house, remotely, from the ASPR. Thursday night, I went into my black box, built for me at the ASPR for the purpose of out-of-body experiments. The black box is a tiny room with a pillow and a rug, where I'm able to sit in complete darkness. I'd then be hooked up to equipment to measure my heart-rate, and various other measuring devices would be used in the next room, monitored by Dr Osis as we communicated via an intercom. Many of these conversations were taped for the case files. Later, we would generally go over the tapes, to then discuss the case with the person who had asked for help.[1]

Once comfortable inside the black box, I informed Dr Osis that Mindy's house dated from 1917. Until Mindy's family moved in, the same family had lived there until the death of an elderly couple, who had been the last residents. When questioned by Dr Osis, I replied that

---

[1] This same method, of Dr Tanous using the black box to relax and focus on information he perceived, was also used during the OBE research conducted by Osis and McCormick (1980). The black box allowed Tanous to go out of his body and travel anywhere he desired, much like remote viewing, but he claimed to actually be there in the astral body (see Auerbach, 1986, for accounts of Dr Tanous' astral travelling abilities; see Introduction by Cooper).

both had died of natural causes, although I seemed less certain about the female. I felt she might have died as a result of over-dosing on medication, perhaps intentionally. In any event, her death had not been easy. Neither of them, I understood, had been very happy.

The woman appeared to be wearing a long dress that reached below her ankles. She spoke to me, repeating over and over, "I did not mean it this way. I must say, it was not meant this way." Small and plump, and in her mid-sixties, she paced before me in what I felt was an attempt to settle the scene, for the elderly couple and the present inhabitants of the house.

Not long after that, I picked up on the collective energy of a scene that had been repeated in an upstairs room of the house. It was the early 1920s. A blonde child about five or six was sitting on a black oak floor in his parents' bedroom as a heated argument raged around him.

"Is the argument between the parents, or between them and the child?" Dr Osis questioned.

I commented briefly, "Between them."

There was a long silence that left Dr Osis waiting.

Finally, I continued: "The man appears to be becoming very violent. He is very angry, in fact. The woman is trying to hold on. I see her rushing over to pick up the child; it seems she is convinced that the man is going to attack the child. I see her holding the child. The man tries to take him from her. The woman is screaming and the child is crying and the man keeps saying, 'Something has to be done, something has to be done.'

Now she is running into a small room adjoining their bedroom where the child is placed on the bed."

Dr Osis asked me to describe the room. I said that it was very dark. There were no windows. It was a small room, hardly big enough for the child and his mother.

I continued: "The man is saying, 'It's for the good of us all.' I guess he wants to put the child away and the woman doesn't want to. I have my doubts that the other children are even allowed to see the child. They may not have seen him at all."

After another long silence, I comment further: "I can see why a child would be frightened staying in such a place. I can hear moaning from the child… I would say this is about six months before the child died." I ended the day's session then, expecting to go back the next day to the same scene and resume my investigations with Dr Osis. But the next afternoon, I found myself in an entirely different situation.

I settled myself back into the black box and began talking over the intercom with Dr Osis:

"There's some kind of structure. It is a small building…" I said with hesitation. "You know, Dr Osis, it is the beginning of the same structure that was completed in 1917. There was some kind of structure on that land, on which a woman had previously died. There are several cross-sections of things."

In the adjoining room, Dr Osis listened with interest. He knew now that we were dealing with multiple manifestations. "What does the woman look like?"

"She's about thirty-five. Dark hair. She wears a bonnet. She's very well dressed. The dress goes, I would say, close to her ankles or just a little above them. So it's not a 1917 scene."

"Can you say more about her?"

"Just…"

"Does she want to tell you something?" Dr Osis questioned.

"At the present time, no. She just seems to be floating."

"Does she want to tell you something that happened to her? Did she die a violent death? A natural death? Perhaps accidental?" Dr Osis probed.

There was a long silence before I spoke. "Dr Osis, this is crazy. I have never seen this before."

"What is it?" Dr Osis was staring at the instruments (i.e., the strain-gauge, heart-rate monitor, etc.). They were giving out unusual readings, at increasing rates.

"It's like a small tombstone. Perhaps the woman was buried there and moved later. Or else she's still buried there. Or maybe she's buried nearby and nobody knows anything about it. It's a tombstone with a mound. She's pointing at it. All green grass, with a mound like a piece of rock. It's not a regular tombstone, Dr Osis. She keeps pointing at it but I don't see any name on it. There's something running through my mind, something like Margaret, but I don't know what that means. It's fading. I'm holding her hand. Is anything happening?"

Dr Osis checked his instruments; the needles were fluctuating at an alarming rate. "Right now, yes," he told me.

"We're talking. She's telling me that there was a dreadful epidemic or disease in which everyone in the village thought she was dead. She was buried alive. She's pointing to the grave." Once again, I stopped abruptly. "Oh my...," my voice expressed great pain. "She was married. At the time she was pronounced dead, she was pregnant and buried alive."

"It must have been terrible to awaken in the grave," Dr Osis said sympathetically, partly for my benefit.

"She is telling me, 'Now I have told you. This completes the event.' She is standing at the foot of her grave talking to me. There's this mound and a slab of rock at the other end. Now she's disappearing; it's as though she's lying down and resting."

The next thing Dr Osis heard was my normal speaking voice: "I'm back, Dr Osis." There were tears streaming down my face.

Two days later, Dr Osis and I told Mindy that her house was haunted by two women: a woman with a child (who had had mental health problems and had died in the house), and the woman who'd died in the smallpox epidemic. On the phone, Mindy confessed that something very odd had happened to her.

She had been sleeping in her room when, all at once, she woke up and looked around. She saw what she described as sparkles in front of her eyes. They shimmered against the wall for several seconds and disappeared. In their place was a dark rectangle that looked like a screen. Mindy watched, fascinated, as a person walked through the screen. When she got out of the bed to investigate, the person vanished. Even though Mindy looked around the room, she couldn't find a trace. Her curiosity satisfied, she turned around to get back into bed and saw a pair of bare feet on the quilt. There was a pretty, dark-haired woman sitting there, weeping. Mindy walked over to the young woman. She didn't touch her, but she consoled her. Eventually, the woman stopped weeping and vanished.

From then on, there were no more incidents in the house. Stevie stopped having nightmares about strange people he'd never seen, in strange rooms he'd never been in. Once the two women, grieving over the fates of their children, had been given the chance to communicate their histories, the manifestations ceased. Perhaps the hauntings had been activated by the presence of a happy, healthy child in the house.

At the further investigations of Dr Osis, the family who had previously occupied the house affirmed the story of the child with mental health issues. Dr Osis discovered from further research that a smallpox epidemic had killed a thousand people in the area during the time I had described.

As I reported in the case files: "Dr Osis says that every time I go into a house I quieten things down. Well, it's part of our research."

Hawk Mountain

One of the best examples of a house with multiple manifestations was demonstrated in the Hawk Mountain case. Hawk Mountain's disturbance evolved from one seminal dramatic incident that took on a momentum of its own and produced a 'spiralling effect,' a process of unleashed psychic energy, unique to certain cases.

For over a century, Hawk Mountain had been drawing certain types of people, attracting individuals to the house who would repeat, in varying degrees, the themes inherent in the core disturbance. The young man living in the house – at the time Dr Osis and I conducted our investigations – was involved with many women at once and had the same name, as well as being the same age, as one of the original occupants.

In 1982, a report was phoned in to Dr Osis from the Audubon Society suggesting he might want to investigate a house in the Poconos that had a long history of supernatural visitations. The house was a study site for the Society, as there are a large number of hawks in the area, and the house had been donated by a woman with an interest in hawks.

The old tavern on the property had become a housing facility for the Audubon curators who worked at the sanctuary. The inn was a squat, stucco-covered fieldstone dwelling with a slate roof. Low beamed ceilings and wide pine floors were beautifully kept by Seth, the young assistant curator. Seth claimed to have seen the kitchen light switch go on and off frequently. His girl-friend had heard a young child crying in the night. There were sounds of footsteps, and bodies being dragged around the house. For several months, the glass doors in the dining room opened and closed violently. When Seth stuck a tab of cardboard in the doors to make them harder to open, they still flew open – with the tab of cardboard carefully in place.

A friend of the curator, who operated the bird-band-ing station, was sleeping in the living-room one night when he was awakened by the sensation of a heavy pres-sure on his chest. The minute he woke up, the feeling was gone. The odd thing was, he found himself stand-ing out on the back porch looking at his watch, real-izing that it was three o'clock in the morning, and he had no idea about how he got there.

Legend had it that, in the mid-1800s, a particularly unscrupulous German owner made it a habit to get the travelling salesmen drunk at the bar as they came through the pass (formerly an Indian trail) on the high-way that the tavern dominated. The salesmen would usually be loaded with goods and, once inebriated out of their senses, the cruel owner would take advantage of their state by dragging them into the woods and be-heading them with an axe. The owner would often be seen hawking the stolen wares, but no charges were ever levelled against him, even though he was said to have murdered 12 men. Soon after he died and was buried, lightning was reported to have struck his grave.

Dr Osis and I arrived at Hawk Mountain on a clear October day. The young curator and his girlfriend had gone away for the weekend in order to enable Dr Osis, Donna McCormick, and myself, to explore the place without interruption. After Dr Osis and Donna had set up equipment around the house, I began my tour of it. As usual, Dr Osis waited for me to make comments and observations, listening calmly and asking for clarifications when he needed them. The house had been visited by several psychics before, but nothing had been laid to rest.

I was tense and nervous, and Dr Osis knew I had seen something already. We sat in the sparsely furnished dining-room around the table, with three cups of coffee and the tape recorder.

When I was ready, I leaned forward to Dr Osis and the tape recorder:

"The energy here is very good," I began tentatively. "But at the same time, inside of that energy there are events which took place that have not been balanced."

"This energy you see is the present occupant?" Dr Osis asked.

I nodded. "The present occupant certainly has something to do with activating that energy at the present time. He is responsible to some degree. There is an indirect relationship to him. I don't quite know how to explain it. It's very new."

"You mean an energy which somebody brings back to life?" Dr Osis asked calmly.

"As you bring up one event, one experience, other experiences are connected to it," I said, quite vaguely.

"You see many events? Lots of imprints connected to this?"

"That's right. The experiences are connected."

"But a similar type of experience?" Donna asked.

"It's a similar type of experience, but it is not the same person. Let me show you what I see. I keep seeing this man riding a horse. He's galloping. The man is very young. This is what I saw outside."

Dr Osis nodded and made notes on the pad in front of him in his small, precise handwriting. "What did the man look like?"

"The man looked... he had a hat on. He's wearing what appears to be a uniform. I see this man stopping in front and coming in here." I rubbed my eyes. "I'm not sure if that's the baseline or the original element. How old is the man who lives here?" I asked.

"He's young," Dr Osis said. "But how old exactly? I'm not really sure."

"The man I saw on the horse is a very young man."

"Some event in the past?"

"Yes. At least a hundred years. At least."

Dr Osis nodded and enquired further: "The man on the horse. Is he the victim of the dramatic event, or did he cause a dramatic event?"

"He is involved in a dramatic event but just how, I don't know at this time. I would have to relive that. There is something lacking here," I said. "Something is missing from the original building. Something like a cooking fireplace. Like an open fire. Now, let me get back into the consciousness of this energy. The interesting thing about all of this, Dr Osis, is that the events that take place here are being attracted by a certain energy. Don't get me wrong. It's not a curse, nothing like that. But things happen in this house because of the energy."

"Like disturbances?" Dr Osis probed.

"Like galloping horses, heavy steps, a cry."

The three of us sat in the silence of the dining-room. Donna started to shiver. After several minutes, I began again: "Another scene that comes into focus, Dr Osis, is a wagon carriage rolling up. Some vehicle with four wheels."

Dr Osis nodded: "Yes, that has been heard quite a bit. Anything happen with the wagon?"

"Yes. Someone got out of the wagon and later died in this place. Apparently, the basis of incidents in this place are related more to a woman than to a man."

Dr Osis had his doubts, but didn't say anything.

"You did see a man riding a horse?" Donna asked.

"Yes," I thought for a moment. "I doubt if a woman living here alone would be happy in this house."

Dr Osis thought back on all the former tenants of the building. "They said so," he said.

"They said they were happy?"

"I talked with one who lived here," Dr Osis said.

"Was she living alone or married?"

"Married."

"That would probably be different."

Dr Osis checked his notes. "I suppose I can understand that. Okay. Let's sum up. You see a young man outside riding a horse. You hear heavy steps upstairs, an impression of a woman and, before, you said somebody had died. Was it violent or natural?"

"Violent." I stood up, put my hands in my pockets, and began walking about the room. "I can almost point to the spot just about here."

"We are in [what used to be] the living-room on the right side of the house," Dr Osis announced, for the benefit of the tape recorder.

I perceived further: "I am willing to say some of the things happened right in here, in the room."

"Now you say somebody was killed," Dr Osis prompted. "Did you see the killer or the victim?"

"This is what I'm going to relive, Dr Osis. It's a member of the family of the owners. That person died violently here. The person who died is about 27 or 28. I have to say he's the same person I first saw galloping on the horse. I also have to say... now I'm seeing the woman. A carriage and a woman betrothed and she learns here in this room that the man she was to marry was killed."

"So she drove in here and discovered that?" Dr Osis asked.

"Yes."

For several moments, I looked out at the cars and trucks whizzing by on the highway outside the house.

The curator's dog began to bark from the backyard. But I didn't notice anything; I was back reliving a scene a hundred years ago.

"She remains and marries," I guessed, before correcting myself. "No, no, that's not it. I'll have to come back to that. I'm trying to balance the energy here now," I explained. "It's something totally different. One of the things I told Dr Osis is that I want to find the origin of the disturbances so I won't tune into a lot of subsequent things. You know," I nodded over at Donna. "You're sitting practically where a lot of these things actually happened. There was an open fireplace right here."

A few minutes later, I added: "There's pressure on my chest."

"On your chest?" Dr Osis asked.

"Yes."

"I've been hurt very badly," I continued. "I am lying on the floor. I mean, I'm reliving the character of this person. It is the young man; the young man is blonde. He is slim, about 5' 10". He has a very light beard. His pants are tight at the bottom and he's wearing what appear to be a vest and a coat. All matching. And some kind of boots."

"Riding breeches?" Donna asked.

"Does any name come to mind?" Dr Osis probed.

"I know that the man's name is a biblical name. In fact, the man carried on his horse one of the few Bibles in the region. I can tell you why the basic disturbance occurred. The person who killed this man was never punished. I mean, nobody ever did anything about it.

One died out of suffering, the other out of guilt. The person who was killed said they would be tied together forever. Unless one was released, the other would never be, either."

I walked around the room, concentrating, and then continued: "May I ask you a question? Did anybody who lived here before have any experiences of something going through the house?"

"Sure."

"There were others?"

"Oh, yes. In what you saw, did you get a glimpse of the killer?" Dr Osis asked gently.

I spoke slowly: "The way the person was killed was with a knife. I can feel now why my chest and stomach were so painful."

"You see a knife or cutting instruments?" Dr Osis asked.

"A knife. In the chest. The person with the knife appears older than the victim. He's bearded. Dark. I'd have to say he's much older than the man on the floor. It's crazy, but I would have to say that he's forty or older."

"That's quite a bit older."

"He is a big man, a heavy man. He's very strongly built. He's not skinny. He looks distinguished, but yet..."

"What is that characteristic you were beginning to tell me?" Dr Osis asked.

"I don't know how to describe it, Dr Osis. He has a mean eye. I don't know if there's something wrong with the eye, but it's something to that effect."

"That would be a good characteristic to note," Dr Osis told Donna.

I was completely caught up in the events I was seeing; it was almost as though Donna and Dr Osis weren't in the room.

"You know something? Why he killed that person? And I know they didn't punish him. The man is a father of a daughter. True or not, I don't know."

"It was not a robbery?" Dr Osis probed.

"No."

Dr Osis began to look through his notes in an attempt to make some kind of sense out of the story I was relating.

"So what caused the murder was the sexual transgression with the mean-eyed man's daughter. Is she the woman who came to look for the man?"

"No, she is not. What I can tell you, Dr Osis, is that the whole basis of the disturbances started here."

"Real or imaginary?"

"Well, the accusation is real, I don't know if the act actually occurred or not. In any case, the man lying on the floor was killed for this. He was killed out of a biblical belief that for such a thing, death was called for. There's moaning and breathing. He lived for a while. I see people trying to take care of him."

"What about the woman who came?" Donna asked.

"Did you get anything about the killer's name?" Dr Osis repeated.

I thought for a few moments. "I'm willing to say that Seth was one of the names."

"Seth? To which man does this name relate?"

"I would say to the man who was killed. And I would also say that the sound of that bird is telling me I'm right," I grinned, as a hawk cried from the blue spruce tree next to the dining-room.

"And the killer?"

"The killer? Well, I'd have to go back into his mind. The affair with his daughter, she was only about 12 or 13 years old."

"So it was a moral offence."

"That's right. I believe that the father's name was something like Isa or Isaiah or Isaac."

I sat down in the chair nearest to Donna.

"You know I don't believe in curses, Dr Osis. For instance, I don't believe that one person can put a hex on someone else. But I do believe that something is still very much present and has caused a lot of related incidents."

"But what you said is that the crimes spiral. That was the phrase you used, a spiralling effect."

"The spiralling thing here means that other events have taken place."

"Of the same nature?" Dr Osis asked.

"I'm not sure. Criminal. I'm sure of that."

Dr Osis nodded thoughtfully. "So this event was the start of it all?"

"Yes, that's right." I agreed. "What has happened is that this crime was committed, this murder.

Apparently, the man who died was somehow attached to his murder."

Suddenly, I became animated. "And I want to tell you something also… oh boy."

"What happened?"

At that moment, Dr Osis and Donna stiffened in the chill that swept through the room. Through the window came the scream of a hawk.

"Are you telling me I'm right?"

I smiled to myself. I jumped up from my chair and headed for the porch where the current caretaker's friend found himself standing in confusion at three o'clock in the morning.

"I'll be right back. But I'll tell you what happened to the man who killed *him*!"

Dr Osis and Donna followed me around the back of the house. They watched as I stood by myself, a little way off from the house, looking down the road towards the highway where trucks careered back and forth along the road. Donna shivered. I began talking to myself. I turned around. I then clasped my hands behind my back and walked to Dr Osis and Donna, my face – sad in expression. The three of us walked back to the living-room.

"The killer was riding down the road away from the house on his horse when something came toward them. It scared the horse. The horse threw the man and he broke his neck."

"A bird or apparition frightened the horse?" Dr Osis started the tape recorder.

"It wasn't an apparition, Dr Osis. It was a great animal cry."

"Horses get frightened," Dr Osis agreed.

"In other words, Dr Osis, the killer was fleeing on his horse and his death was his punishment. The man he had killed had not done anything to his daughter. It appears as though, in the transcendence of his death, the killer discovered he was wrong."

"I see. Now, as I remember, the first thing you saw when you came up the stairs was something like an energy spiral, right?" Dr Osis questioned.

"Yes. There were other incidents that followed, but this was the first."

"Sometimes they say that when a bull smells blood he goes to the next victim, too. Something like that?" Dr Osis asked.

"That's right. Then something or someone came into the house and did something, and for a while the disturbances stopped. But what I'm getting, Dr Osis, is that they began again with Seth, the new caretaker who is living here now."

"I see," Dr Osis commented. "There certainly was a drama here and a very nasty one. But let me understand that spiral. You asked me if I understood what you were trying to explain to me and I didn't. You say that the crime occurred in an atmosphere of revenge and hate, and spread somehow to the people in this house who perpetuated crimes again. That's the idea?"

"That's right," I paused, and added: "I have a feeling that the man who was frightened, who got his neck broken, has been seen. I don't know what Seth saw, he must have had some heavy things happening around here."

"You mean," Dr Osis clarified in an attempt to understand, "there were relationships around here having to do with Seth, the current curator, that brought this all back?"

"That's right."

"Those were the conclusions I had come to myself," Dr Osis agreed.

"And before that, the original crime worked as a curse on the family, drawing them into this pattern of death and murder."

"And the woman you saw?"

I walked around the room.

"After the murder, the girl drove up in a carriage. She was very young, maybe 17, and she was supposed to marry the man lying dead on the floor. She never recovered from the incident. She remained here, Dr Osis, and became a prostitute. She died here giving birth to a child. I'm heavy with energy, Dr Osis. There are chills running up and down my spine."

"Certainly," Dr Osis decided, "if she knew how he was killed and why, it would be even more torturing. Certainly a dramatic scene. The disturbances after that depend on the original situation, the one we've been discussing. Am I correct in that assumption?"

31

"That's right, the whole family was caught in this thing."

"So the legend about the murdering innkeeper seems to be definitely off-beam. They're not consistent."

I smiled.

"Everyone likes a legend, Dr Osis. With legends of people being killed in taverns, well, you find this all the time. But if we are looking at what I relived for this place, it doesn't mean it couldn't have happened later, after the baseline event."

"You see connecting shadows hovering about a central event such as this and that's what is causing a kinetic... you mentioned a woman?" Dr Osis asked.

"She remained here," I replied.

"The attacked woman?"

"She lived someplace else."

"Are you cold?"

"There is a great deal of pressure in this room," I said.

"That's what people claim."

"I feel cold," Donna said, "but I didn't think it was anything, I thought it was just the altitude."

"No," Dr Osis corrected.

"I'm really freezing and there is a great deal of pressure. My eyes, my whole body. There's a freezing in my back and pressure in my chest," I paused. "I don't know what people are feeling, but I'm feeling the pressure to the point that it's really physically affecting me."

"It's an oppressed feeling?"

"Yes. Tired. Sleepy. I feel drawn."

"Your feeling was that the crime somehow holds the victim and the killer in this place. But you said the killer was causing the disturbances?"

"That's right. The killer is the one who believes there is something going on, between the killer's daughter and the man on the floor. The crime occurred because the killer was avenging a sexual incident, so any sexual thing... would reactivate new rage," I finished.

"You said you heard a woman's voice, or didn't you?" Dr Osis queried.

"Yes, the woman who travelled here. Screams, moaning, a lot of commotion. She travelled a long way to get here. The girl never recovered from the incident and she became a prostitute, as I said before."

"So very hard," Dr Osis' voice was soft with empathy. "Her life was killed, so to speak."

"Yes."

"And you know something else, Dr Osis, the heaviest thing here besides the killing is sexual energy. What is amazing is that after the death of her father, the girl who had accused the young man of rape came out and admitted it wasn't true – that she had made the whole thing up."

"And," Dr Osis volunteered, "this boy named Seth, the curator who had the same name as the boy accused of rape, was having girls over here and reviving the whole story. He's single, and about the same age as the boy who was killed. From the initial event, people in the family got caught up in the spiralling energy."

I worked at the house for several weeks reconciling the killer and his victim. As I later told the story (corroborated by newspaper reports of the time), the inn had been owned by a German family whose son had been in love with a 17-year-old girl.

They became lovers and planned to be married, but when the woman drove up in the carriage, she found her betrothed dead on the floor. When she found out why, she was destroyed. The local schoolmaster's daughter had accused the young man of rape. As the girl was only 12 or 13 at the time, nobody thought of questioning her. She had been lying, and nobody thought to question her. However, she didn't tell the truth until it was too late. Her father rode off and killed Seth where he was waiting at the bar for his fiancé. Seth, in his dying moments, cursed the girl's father, telling the man he had never raped his daughter and that they'd be locked in death for the rest of time.

Before Seth died, the murderer's horse was spooked by a hawk on the road and the schoolmaster fell off his horse, broke his neck and died. Seth had been right. The two men were united in death. They both haunted the house. Upstairs, the ghost of the young woman disturbed the bedroom where she later died in childbirth. Her instantly orphaned child – who suffered from mental health issues, as well as being deaf – subsequently died at the young age of 12 and haunted the house as well. Meanwhile, the entire downstairs was populated by ghosts of the merchants killed by the innkeeper.

When Dr Osis and I finally left Hawk Mountain, the inn was at peace and Seth had only the hawks to contend with. The 'spiralling effect' I related to Dr Osis had included, in all, perhaps 28 apparitions.

3

CONTINUED BONDS

I have encountered many instances of ghosts of individuals who had loved each other so completely
in life that they'd promised to meet beyond the
grave. Sometimes the lovers died in different times or
places, in dramatically charged emotional situations.
When unable to find the person for whom they were
waiting, they began to prowl houses or sites in an end-
less search.

In 1983, I went to investigate such a case in a house
set in the lush Pennsylvania farm country. The then
residents of the house were by nature practical and
down-to-earth, hardly the kind of people who would
be carried away by their imagination. But they could no
longer rationally explain the activity in the farmhouse

even though they had tried to ignore it for months. Doors opened and slammed shut, footsteps could be heard on the stairs, and the inhabitants of the house would suddenly be overcome by cold chills. Furniture moved around in the upstairs bedroom and favourite objects went astray in the living-room, never to be found again.

During the 1800s, on the site of a stop on the underground railroad where slaves were sheltered on their way North, a young couple in their early twenties had lived in the house together. They had been very much in love. That was all the family knew about the history of the house.

I began by walking slowly through the interior, starting in the kitchen and moving to the upstairs bedroom. I felt cold chills as I got closer to the bedroom but, once I walked into the room itself, I felt myself in the presence of someone sweet and gentle.

As I walked back downstairs to the living-room, I began to get a sense of someone else downstairs, waiting impatiently in an atmosphere of overwhelming sadness. I returned to the kitchen again and, in a process which I have often described as watching a movie, began to see a beautiful young girl, her hair tied away from her face, her sleeves rolled up and skirts bunched around her waist. The girl was warming a pan of food on the stove and, as I watched, helpless to do anything, the grease spattered into the fire and the pan burst into flame. Horrified, the girl turned around and tried to put out the fire but it was no use. Minutes later, her clothes were burning and the young woman was on fire.

By the time her husband came home that evening, there was nothing more to be done. He picked her up and carried her into their bedroom where, two days later, she died. But just before her death she managed to tell him how much she loved him. She promised she'd wait in the house for him until he died.

The young man grew old in the house and never remarried. As she'd promised, his wife visited him, particularly late at night when he sat in the living-room reading. To make sure he knew she was there, she moved objects around the room and playfully blew out the candles. He lived alone until his death, helping slaves across the border and keeping later and later hours. After his death, the house became more active than ever, particularly the living-room where it seemed some imaginary thing was ransacking the place for something it was determined to find.

I discovered the young man's ghost, grown elderly now, waiting for his wife in the living-room where she had visited him so often during his life. Meanwhile, her ghost was lingering in the master bedroom. They were both, as they had promised each other, waiting in the house. But, because they had died in different times – forty years apart – they couldn't find each other. The young woman visited the living-room searching for her husband but he was no longer there. He was, instead, frantically searching for her in a different time period.

The first thing I did was to speak to the woman. I explained that her husband hadn't abandoned her at all. On the contrary, he'd been waiting for her downstairs for many years. Then I brought her into her husband's time so they could be together. Because the family currently living in the house had gotten used to the ghosts, they asked me to let them stay and to this day, the ghosts are still there living happily together.

In a haunted house in Lichfield, Connecticut, I encountered another pair of lovers, but, because of the situation surrounding their deaths, they were more violent in communicating their distress at being separated than the gentle ghosts of the peaceful Pennsylvania countryside.

When asked to the house, I found a restored farmhouse decorated in a woodland Indian theme. The refurbished upstairs bedrooms were full of war tomahawks, Indian rugs, quill baskets, small drums, and strings of beads. For no apparent reason, Indians would drift in and out of the house to visit the family currently living there, bringing gifts.

After I was shown through the house, Denise, a small dark-haired woman in her late 30s, and Denise's mother and father sat around a sturdy oak table in the kitchen and talked to me. As I listened to their description of the events that lead them to call the ASPR, I began to get a sense of the house and its surroundings.

Denise was animated and friendly and she tried to make a point of remembering as much as she could for my benefit. "In 1969, this place came on the market and I immediately snapped it up because I wanted land on all four sides of my house. I was tired of being crowded in," Denise explained. "The people moved out and I decided to have my brother, who works for a paint company, come down with sprayers and just redo the whole house white. That way, I could just come in whenever I wanted to, on my own time, and do my own decorating."

"So he came down with two or three of his friends and the big paint sprayers. One of the guys was upstairs doing the bedroom and the door kept shutting on him. Finally, he went downstairs and told my brother that something strange was going on upstairs. 'Somebody didn't like him painting that room', was how he explained it." Denise took a sip of coffee and folded her hands on the table.

"Well, they all went up and told him he'd been drinking too much beer and they helped him finish painting the room. They didn't have any trouble. I moved my stuff in and nothing was going on, and then I took my mother up there." Denise smiled at her mother, who smiled back. "She walks in and the first thing she says is: 'There's someone else in the house'." Denise and her mother laughed.

"So, I say, 'Yeah, Ma you're going through one of your things again, right?' You see," Denise looked across the table at me, "I didn't want to deal with any weird things because I'm this complete sceptic."

"She was friendly," Denise's mother joined in. "I knew it was a *she* right off. The cat could see her."

"That's right. Ma had this old Siamese cat..."

"It was a friendly feeling," Denise's mother ran her fingers along the surface of the oak table. "I always spoke to her."

Denise waited for her mother to say more but, when she didn't, Denise continued. "So, anyway, my sister Diana, who is younger than me, and her girlfriend and a boy from Nebraska named Carl used to get the Ouija board out. They could work that Ouija board like you wouldn't believe. I mean, they'd come out with two or three things every time, right?"

Denise's mother nodded.

"So, they were in here playing with it one night," Denise said, indicating the kitchen, "and I say, 'Okay, if you guys are so great, tell me the name of whatever it is that's been wandering around the house.'" The board told them this girl's name was Beatrice and she had died in a fire in the area and now lived out in this maple tree. So I don't know; I checked with the people who'd lived here before and they said no one had died in the house itself, but that the old barn had burnt down and there were charred beams and things up in the attic. Anyway, there was a maple tree way up on the knoll out there, which had been struck by lightning a while ago. I don't know why, but my sister kept insisting the fire had killed this Beatrice," Denise took in a deep breath.

"It went on like that for weeks. They'd talk to her through the Ouija board, we'd live our lives, and I figured: So Beatrice is around, so what? But then I had this experience with her. I have a long bedroom up in the main section of the house that goes toward the attic, and I was fixing the ceiling. We had a darkroom up there. We got a little carried away but, anyway, a piece of the ceiling fell down. I was planning to seal up the ceiling because it was getting to be spider time, and I knew I was going to have spiders in my bedroom if I didn't seal it off. So I did seal it off, but ten minutes later, the board was down again. I put it up again. I really nailed it tight. Two days later, it was down again. The third time, I put it up there and it came right back down. I stood in the middle of that bedroom and I said: 'Look, Beatrice, do you have a problem, or what? You obviously don't want me to shut off the attic, so I'll tell you what I'm going to do. I'm going out to the main section of the storeroom and I'll open up the back section of the attic so you can get outside, okay? But you should leave my ceiling alone because if I don't seal this off, I'm going to have spiders down in my bedroom and I have this fear of spiders'."

Denise started to giggle. "I couldn't believe I was standing in the middle of an empty room having this conversation. Anyway, I put the board back up on the ceiling and this time it stuck. No problem. Sometime later, my mother was with me and my older brother. He's even more sceptical about all of this than I am."

Denise's mother agreed.

"He thinks it's all 'female imagination', but had just experienced something. He'd been in the bathroom shaving, with mother telling him about the latest episode with Beatrice while he gave her a lecture about how all of that wasn't possible. All of a sudden, this picture hanging on the bathroom wall falls onto the floor, and my brother ends up flying over to the other side of the dining-room and he tells me to go in there. We take a look. The only way that picture could have come off of the wall is if somebody had lifted it off and dropped it."

Denise's father chuckled.

"That's another thing, my father could always sense Beatrice when he was sitting over there at the kitchen table."

"She read the paper with me," her father added.

"Yeah, he gets the Brunswick paper and he's always reading the obits. Every time he'd get to the obituary section, he'd feel something looking over his shoulder. The Ouija board told us Beatrice was looking for someone named Gordon."

"After a while, I stopped reading the paper in the kitchen," her father added.

"We couldn't find out who Gordon was. She wouldn't talk about him."

"Could you identify him with the fire?" I asked.

"No. She kept calling it 'The Great Fire'. She said he had had to save books, something like that. We had years of her pranks. We got used to it. When something happened, we'd turn around and say, 'Well, Beatrice is at it again'. The Ouija board said there was another person involved in all this named Ajax. Ajax came and told us that there was a bad spirit coming because of Beatrice, and that this bad spirit objected to the friendliness Beatrice had developed with us. The next thing that happened was on my sister-in-law's birthday. In May?" Denise asked her mother.

"April."

"Right. Everybody was over and it was a beautiful day out, not one drop of rain. We were all having a good time when all of a sudden, there was lightning, followed by a big crash. We looked out. The maple tree had fallen over. In the last three years, I'd taken all these pictures of the maple tree because it was a fantastic tree. Well, after it was struck by lightning, every picture we had of that tree disappeared. We have nothing to document the plainest fact that there was even a tree there once, other than through the neighbours, who had three cows killed when the tree fell on them," Denise paused for a moment, and then continued.

"That night, nobody wanted to do the Ouija board. They tried it again a few days later but it was a long time before they could get it to work. They got messages from Ajax and Beatrice, all garbled until Beatrice told them to not try to contact them anymore."

Denise's father leaned forward, cupping his elbows in his hands.

"I don't believe in Ouija boards. I'm sceptical about communicating with people on the other side, and with spirits. But there is definitely a female presence in this house. She warned me one time."

"Did this warning take place prior to the tree going down or after?" I asked.

"After. Just before that article came out in the paper about the house being haunted."

"May I ask you one question?" I asked. "The fire in the barn, what was that all about?"

"One day the neighbours who lived next door before we moved in were burning a section of the old barn and it spread to the house."

"And," I wondered, "You said Beatrice said something about going back for books?"

"She said 'I went back', and there were two or three letters no one could make out and then 'books' came. We just assumed she went back for books."

"So, the last time you really felt Beatrice was a year or two ago?"

Denise's father shook his head. "I sleep downstairs here in the corner so I don't have to climb the stairs. This last winter she hasn't been around much. There isn't a strong feeling of her. But the feeling would be just as strong as the feeling of all you people here. I would know that there was somebody and I was never frightened."

"Alright," I stood up. "I would like to see the room where she was felt first. Maybe I can pick her up from the stronger areas and we can come back here. What I usually do is the same thing I do from the laboratory," I explained. "I go to the room where the entity or spirit was first felt and, because all entities have energy where they are, we can see if we can pick up on anything. Right now she's here. I don't know whether we can make contact with her personally or not. What I'm going to do now is relive whatever Beatrice wants to tell me."

Denise and I walked up to the bedroom, and then I went into the middle of the room. Denise leaned against the door frame, her arms folded across her chest, watching. When I started talking again, my voice became calm, and slow.

"First of all, the name Beatrice is only because it is an American name given to her. She's an Indian. She was betrothed to an American man named Gordon. He was a preacher. They ran away together and escaped to this area, do you follow what I'm trying to say? Apparently there was an Indian reservation here. They were caught and killed by Indians. Her spirit is very, very old; she has been looking for him all of this time. She knew this was the last place she ever saw him. He was tied to a tree and whipped. Perhaps struck by lightning. She watched him being burnt and then she was killed. That's why you have her here looking for Gordon.

Gordon had been taken away, but she stayed here. I don't know whether or not she's buried here. This area was covered with a lot of woods." I thought for a moment, and then continued. "There should be a marker somewhere. Have you found daffodils or anything in the field around, an unusual wildflower? Something that grew over and over again, every year?"

Denise shrugged, "Not that I know of."

I walked around the room for a while.

"Now Ajax, by the way, let's get back to Ajax. He's the Indian who helped them escape. Beatrice is not the young woman's real name; Gordon gave it to her because her name was an odd long name. Gordon lived on an Indian reservation and appears to have been teaching something. It's almost like he was a missionary of some kind. He fell in love with this 18- or 19-year-old Indian girl. He wanted to marry her. The tribe all said No, so with the help of Ajax, Beatrice and Gordon decided to leave. But the family of the girl started to track them down and found them here. Perhaps the reason Beatrice is attached to the maple tree is because that was the tree where they burnt Gordon. Anyway, you have Ajax, Gordon, and Beatrice, and they were all young people. And you have your younger sister and her best friend and Carl having conversations with the ghosts. And...," I gestured around the room, "...you have all of the Indian things – to them it's normal. These relationships are not made under ordinary circumstances. There's an attraction inherent to these things."

48

Denise looked puzzled. "But why did Ajax tell us there was an evil thing coming because of Beatrice?"

"From what I can gather, Gordon was tied to the tree and burnt at the tree, alright? I don't know the Indian background for burning people but it appears this boy was burnt. Now, whether they believed – if I'm interpreting right – that he was an evil spirit that they had to do away with, well, Ajax would still remember Gordon as an evil spirit. And he's still here, too. I mean, he doesn't leave, either. Remember, the only reason Beatrice is staying here is because she says she's looking for Gordon. But Gordon may not be able to find her. They died at two different times. Gordon was in ashes before she was killed; she was killed afterwards. The understanding has to be made between the spirit and the soul. Her life is different from her spirit. Her spirit is still tied to the energy of the trauma. You can photograph that with cameras."

I paced the room, thinking out loud anything I perceived on the matter. "Ajax doesn't know either. He doesn't come through on this at all, only Beatrice and Gordon. She was a very pretty girl, maybe 5' 7" in height. Beautiful black hair tied back in pigtails and ribbon patterns down the front. Her dress is made completely out of beads. She was able to walk very softly and lightly. She's buried somewhere around here. Beatrice's energy is held here by that dramatic episode. There's a young man aged about 29 or 30, with a book. He's tied to a tree. Can you imagine the force of the emotions?

Beatrice was held there, forced to watch him burn. It's no wonder she's still roaming around looking for him. The death was unjust and Beatrice is trying to right the imbalance. That's all."

After Denise and I went back to the kitchen, I united Beatrice and her lover and the Litchfield Ghost was gently put to rest. Denise admitted later that she missed Beatrice during the long summer nights when Beatrice used to talk to them on the Ouija board.

54

Psionic Reunion

A Century's Worth of Residents Convene At Beckett's Castle

By Lynne Campbell

tion. "Mr. Beckett belonged to no church, but was not without specific and pronounced ideas regarding the life beyond, which may be characterized as _____. He never used the words

"Yes, there are ghosts here," Mr. Lins says. "Many of them." As we walked through the castle on a sunny September afternoon, he recalled his experiences.

Pointing to a nail in the wall above the kitchen stove, Mr. Lins began. "Four times I hung a painting on that nail," he

lenses with extra-sensory perception (ESP), including clairvoyance (psychic vision), telepathy (mental communication), psychometry (knowledge gained through an associated object), and out-of-body experiences.

Dr. Tanous holds six collegiate _____ He has written two books: *Is _____*

times," he said. "And I have to say that the vibes are excellent. There is no evil in this house.

"I keep hearing motions of people walking. Heavy breathing appears also. And cold chills.

"I'm picking up a man about sixty-five. He is wandering, apparently from

---

Parapsychology is a sensitive subject to many — the believers and the skeptics. The following article is based on the writer's in-depth interviews with Dr. Karlis Osis of the ASPR in New York City and psychic, Dr. Alex Tanous.

Psychic Phenomena... ESP and Apparitions

BY DIANE B. SAXTON

Dr. Alex Tanous is one of two psychics in the U.S. said to possess the pow of light projection, the ability to project light from one's eyes. (This claim not verified by the ASPR.)

"Nothing today is impossible — nothing!" declared Maine Police

centrates on the study of paranormal phenomena, such as extrasensory _____ _____ ___ _____

laboratory. Sometimes his assistar with crime detection work origina in the laboratory often with fi

---

Alex Tanous in the News

Dr Karlis Osis

4

DANDY HOUSE AND FROLIC HOUSE

Note: *This short chapter is an account of Dr Tanous' investigations of the Dandy House poltergeist, alongside his colleague Father Trabold, and also of the Frolic House case. The Dandy House case is a useful example of some of the characteristics and behaviour Dr Tanous displayed when working in haunted locations as a psychic and an investigator. Both of these reports were extracted from a collection of Dr Tanous' notes on his personal accounts of such investigations, of working with the police on psychic crime detection, and of working with people who had had OBEs.*

Although Dr Tanous was sceptical of possessions and exorcisms, it is demonstrated in the Dandy House case that he would not dismiss outright those within the church or religious circles who wished to explore such ideas. But he has made it clear in previous statements that these issues are more religiously driven and psychological than anything else. An exorcism may act much like a placebo, in which the suggestion is given that activity within a house will be made to stop by blessing it, and as a result, the occupants unconsciously dismiss bangs and cracking noises throughout the building, which were once interpreted as 'paranormal'. However, this is just one explanation; each case of a haunting – as Dr Tanous generally agreed – must be judged on its merits, without generalization or prejudice.

Ask any personal counsellor to enumerate the challenges particular to psychological or psychiatric healing and he or she will ultimately tell you that until a counsellor can see a client's problem as if through the client's own eyes, there can be no healing.

So how does one go about counselling those whose compulsive or troublesome behaviour continues to manifest beyond death? The answer is, healing occurs in the same way, whether such personal counselling takes place before or after the demise of the physical body.

Confession is always good for the soul, especially for those spirits who feel a desperate need to tell their poignant personal stories. The timelessness of the *out-of-body* enables me to see where such troubled spirits are coming from, and frees me to be where they are. The Dandy expedition was one such unforgettable case in point.

The Dandy estate was located in a quiet little upstate New York town. Over the years, this sedate homestead had become the meeting place of choice for some rather disquieting spirits. The presence of at least one poltergeist had already been confirmed some five years prior to my arrival. My goal and that of my colleague, Father Alphonsus Trabold of St. Bonaventure University, was to investigate these restless spirits and, if possible, to rid the house of them once and for all.

"The disturbances began as noise without action," explained the homeowner. "The sound of a window slamming when no window could possibly have slammed... things falling, when they really didn't fall. Then we had action without noise," he continued. "A lamp breaking, and we didn't hear anything. Finally, some kind of creature jumped on Beth (a young girl who lived in the house). I think that's what frightened me most."

Soon after I entered the century-old house, I felt spirits there. Father Trabold and I made our way through the rooms with a tape recorder ready. As I acquainted myself with my surroundings, I became more and more absorbed in the house's history until finally its tumultuous past began to speak through me.

"Birds quiet," my recorded statement began. "A girl lying in bed, calling for help, getting no response from her mother and father who are arguing. I am now *very* cold. The chill is getting even stronger. The birds will remain quiet as I leave and draw the energy from the room. There are other energies in the room which are also affecting me. The vibrations are of certain things that have disquieted her over the years... The other energy is that of a girl... oh, I would say 12 or 13 – who was raped and killed. The young girl was raped by a man who was a bachelor... Again, the chills are hitting me...

I'm picking up a young man, 18 or 19, who was killed in an accident. For some reason, all these energies are converging here. There's also been the death of a man in this room, a death which was a drastic death of agony – not a murder or a suicide.

What I am going to do now is pick up all of this energy... Alright, the energy has now been picked up. As you see, the lights go out. The energy is forcing me to say that it does not want to leave. The energy is here but... her fiancé had a very tragic death. The energies are sorrowful energies. Tragic. The person – the man – drowned and the woman has never gotten over it. The woman locked herself in this room from time to time and would not come out at all..."

At this point I began conversing directly with the spirits or energies involved, directing them to release their sorrows and in so doing to release their consciousness from the confines of the house.

"You must, you must, you must… time has gone, a child cannot be born. I am going to force you, force you. You must leave. The answer is No, you cannot stay. You cannot stay. (Heavy breathing, gasping, was audible on the tape at this point). Alright, alright, let's go. Let's go. Alright."

Now the energy reached out to make physical contact with me.

"The burn is there. I know you burned me. I realize it. But I'm going to take you with me, no matter what happens. I'm holding on to you. Go ahead. No you're not. You're not going to take over. I'm going to have you. Alright, going? Let's go. Let's go. I want to break you, break you (gasping – audible on the tape)."

Later, Father Trabold described what I had been through, from his point of view:

"At first, you were speaking in a very calm way, sort of commenting on the different vibrations you got. Then, all at once, you stopped for a moment, and suddenly you were completely unaware of us. You started talking to the entity that was there – a young blind girl. It was obvious that the spirit didn't want to leave. You were saying with more force each time that it should leave, and then parts of your body began to contort, especially your face, and your hands. You began to sway and sort of fall backward, and I put my arms around you and began to hold you. The weight was almost more than

I could hold. The force was putting up a tremendous battle but you didn't give up."

After my attempt to direct the spirits away from the Dandy house, Father Trabold performed an exorcism. Evidently, our combined efforts worked. The poltergeist activity ceased forever. The burn that I spoke of on the tape? It was real alright. When I unbuttoned my shirt, I found a raw red patch on my side about the size and shape of a 50-cent piece.

ॐ

On 15 January, 1983, I was a guest at the home of George 'Frolic', in Weymouth at the Big Bend in Chadds Ford, Pennsylvania.

Shortly after I arrived, I went to the ground floor where the kitchen and a large dining area were located. I walked into the dining room and stopped as I sensed happenings from many years before. I said, "George Washington was here, and the floor was then dirt."

Frolic said, "You are standing where we found an Indian buried, and when we fixed this room we left him in the place we found him."

Mr Frolic also said that Washington had written to his wife about this place; but that he doubted if Washington visited here as this had been a loyalist house. I had also heard that the seat which Martha Washington sat on while having her portrait painted was on the second floor of this house.

I was a guest in the Frolic house for several days, and one evening as I sat on a chair with my feet near where the skeleton was, I felt a cold chill and suddenly saw the whole story unfold in my mind, like a movie. It was apparent to me that the bones in the grave were not those of an Indian, but of a 16-year-old boy who had been in Washington's army. I saw that the boy was very close to Washington, and did many little chores for him – like shining shoes, etc.

The boy seemed to be suffering from a fever which he could not handle and it was getting worse. The boy confessed to General Washington that he was a runaway and that he knew the loyalist family living in the Bend, and that they would help him if he went to them. It was apparent to me that it was really the boy's sweetheart who was living in the house with her parents and brother.

General Washington gave his permission and the boy went to the house and was met by the family there. They realized that he was very sick, and tried to help him. The fever would not break. A day or two after he arrived at the house, he died.

He had told the family that he was in the area with Washington's army. The girl then took the risk of going to see Washington to tell him what had happened. Because of the boy's devotion, Washington himself escorted the girl back to the house and identified the body. Because of the hot weather, the boy was buried here. Washington wrote and signed a paper which he gave to these people to give to the parents of the boy. This paper has never been destroyed. I believe that it is still in existence.

5

GHOSTS, SOULS,
AND SPIRITS?

Note: *The following chapter was taken from a transcript of an interview carried out with Dr Tanous on 11 December, 1981. It is a rare personal insight into Dr Tanous' views on hauntings, spirits, and also, on characteristics of ghosts.*

The first part of the interview briefly discusses the rarely debated topic of ghosts and ethnicity. This follows on with personal views on the reality of ghosts, and then the more theological debate – which is often discussed, more so within the USA – of demonic possession, in relation to ghosts.

The majority of the interview had taken place within the framework of casual speech and therefore the initial transcript – from the Alex Tanous Foundation files – did not make complete sense in places. Therefore, it has been edited for clarity, as far as is possible from general speech, without changing the original thoughts and opinions of the interviewer or of Dr Tanous.

⟳

Tanous: For the first time, last week I had my first black ghost. I had not seen black ghosts before on the personal level of investigation.

Interviewer: What is a black ghost?

Tanous: A person that's black and not white. Usually, it's a white person who calls us in. It's rare that we have a call from black people who have ghosts in their house.

Interviewer: Where was the call?

Tanous: The New York area. And I found out that there were two ghosts. And with one of them, we were able to verify that it was the mother of the woman who lived in the house – I think the woman was 39 and had a child. The ghost had a relationship to the son. But she was not from the house. She had died somewhere else, and was a 'visiting ghost' as I call them. And the other ghost was her brother – but we cannot verify that as yet – who had been separated from his sister; after their mother's death he had been adopted by someone else. So the only thing that we could come up with was that he was her brother, but that needs verification.

If these entities are who we believe they are and I've come up with the right answer, then the ghost will balance itself out. By balance itself out, I mean it will quieten down, because they tell their story.

Interviewer: You mean the ghosts are there just until someone recognizes them?

Tanous: Yes, recognizes them, and then they tell me that they are visiting. That's all. And then after that, that's it. The current occupant was six years old when the mother died. She was subsequently adopted by someone else and...

Interviewer: So this was a different house?

Tanous: A different house completely. The other was somewhere in the south. And now they're living in New York. These ghosts are 'visiting ghosts'.

Interviewer: Why did they call you?

Tanous: To find out if it's true or not. If the ghosts were their imagination or not.

Interviewer: They saw the ghosts?

Tanous: What they saw was someone coming closer, lights, all sorts of manifestations, footsteps, the regular change of weather, I mean, change of climate and so forth. There is so much of these things that we're looking into now with ghost-hunting, and we do need it for our research. Other cases we get sent are to do with police cases, but that is of course very much confidential...

Tanous: Do ghosts exist? I personally believe that ghosts exist. What are they? Are they a proof of survival? The work that I am doing is certainly to show whether there is proof for survival. Now, what would activate a ghost? These are all questions of great interest. And how do you recognize a ghost?

There are manifestations of ghosts that are visible to one person alone. They may see something out of the corner of their eye, or something appearing in the room, or passing by, but only one person is seeing it. When only one person is seeing it, it's extremely hard for any verification. But I will visit the house to see if this 'ghost' does exist. What I do is this. When I go into a house, nothing is told to me – about the house or about the manifestations. I go there 'blindfolded' so to speak, not blindfolded literally, and I go through the house and see what I can find – whether there is a ghost – and then give my report. Then, we talk to the people about it.

Now, there are several things one must observe when one goes into a haunted house.

Could it be telekinetic? Meaning, could the people in the house cause objects to move or things to happen. If there is an emotional problem in the house, it may cause objects to move, which might not be caused by a ghost. Or it may cause objects to fall. If there are young children in the house, their presence may also result in a telekinetic effect; they may be causing it by their own minds, consciously or unconsciously.

Interviewer: You mean young children have more telekinetic powers than adults?

Tanous: Oh certainly. That's why young children can sometimes bend spoons; they do a lot of things, and can even activate ghosts. There was a case, I think, in Virginia, where a boy aged eight or nine – it was reported – upset a whole house without realizing it. He had everything upside down; thus, it was investigated.

Other people might think that it's demonic. I've never found a house possessed by demonic ghosts. I've never found what I would call an evil ghost. No possessive ghosts. Mischievous ghosts, yes, where they would move objects when the person was gone, and this was later realized. But as far as harming someone, no. Now, there is some literature that claims that some of this has happened. I would have to study that literature and find out exactly what was the harm to the person. It's hard for me to believe an entity would do that. I've never found...

Interviewer: But people do that. People harm each other.

Tanous: Yes. But I couldn't see ghosts doing that. Ghosts will not harm people, though they may move objects and hide them. And to the point that some have even burnt houses down. But harm to another person, or possession of another person, I've never seen that. You know, cutting somebody else, or physical harm. One can imagine that a person having this experience could, through his or her own mind, cause a lot of these things. But, personally I have not – at least not in my research for a number of years, working with the ASPR – ever found any evidence for this.

Let's look at 'How we sense a ghost'. Usually, a change in temperature in the house. If hot, it will be very cold in places. We do hear footsteps and knocks. True, some of these have to be investigated quite closely, as to whether there are ghosts, or just natural cracking and creaks in the house.

One haunted house we were visiting in Maine had had fires three times on one side of the house. I took a group there, and I found out that it had originally been burned by an Indian, because the land had something to do with their land. Strangely enough, when the house was first burned by an Indian, it was owned by a seaman, and his child and wife had died in the fire; yet when a later owner – a woman – rebuilt it for the third time, the inside of the house was built like a ship, and the woman knew nothing about that past.

And then we went through the whole house, sensed the cold, and heard footsteps on the stairs. So we asked the photographer to take a picture, a series of pictures of the stairs, and the imprint of the footstep on the stairs can be seen. We have it on film. So ghosts do have a physical effect.

Interviewer: What about smells?

Tanous: Smells are another thing reported in haunted locations. Flowers. Cooking. Smoke. You know, pipe tobacco, and stuff like that. Smells that don't naturally belong there. There are certain characteristics which are very strong, like if you go into a house and smell a flower which isn't there. And my role then is to find out if these things are true. Now, how do I make contact? How do I know? And, what do I do? To be honest, there is very little I can do. It is all done through my astral body, 'Alex 2'.

Just like in the OBE studies with Dr Osis, I am able, at will, to leave my body, and meet them on *their* level. With my personal consciousness, combined with the consciousness of Alex 2, the two of us are able to contact the ghosts. I would call it 'ghost,' and I'll clarify that a little later.

Different types of occurrences might then happen. They may talk to me. Tell me what's going on. Or they will show me something like a movie. We relive the scene that has taken place. Like the one in Maine: I relived the scene where the woman was sitting in her chair, rocking her child, the house burning, her husband coming back and finding the house burnt. So he is looking still for his wife and child. We found no burial ground or anything else, but remember we're now in the late 1600s or 1700s, so it was not as evident a burial as we have, so he's constantly looking, and that's why the current occupants heard footsteps. That's why the woman living there was able to see the rocking chair rock back and forth, and other manifestations, but they were real, and the pictures prove that they are there. So these things happen.

I have to make a distinction here between the spirit and the soul. I want to call spirit, 'personality'. And soul, 'individuality'. In other words the soul makes you an individual; we're getting into the philosophical here, but trying to get into the modern terminology. If life leaves your body, you die. If your spirit leaves your body, you do not die. These spirits, as far as we can see, are energy, and are still in some way earthbound, it has nothing to do with the individuality. It has to do with an experience, here and now, that *took* place, the burning of the house, the man *looking* for that person. Or a murder taking place that needs to be retold, or an event *taking* place that we have to balance. It's that, which I would call 'ghost' or 'spirit'.

There's also the individuality, the 'apparition' – this is where the individuality comes over and speaks to you.

Interviewer: So there you're talking about 'soul'?

Tanous: I'm talking about someone who has transcended, someone who is a person who has a soul, after death. In the past, with any type of survival, they said that it was a survival of personality. Yes, in the individuality there is a personality survival. You will still be 'Brad' or 'Mary' in the afterlife. What I'm talking about here is a personality in an experience, such as an incident taking place... usually the incident that they play out is something someone has to know about – that someone's been buried alive, murdered, and so on. Or if there is a separation involved in one of these personalities, it visits as a ghost because there are people there whom they've been separated from, and want to see again. You know, over miles. Is it possible that the individuality would visit the house, too, from a distance; the answer is Yes.

Interviewer: Well, with the black mother in the house, she was a visiting ghost?

Tanous: Yes. But the incident did not happen in the house.

Interviewer: Well how does that fit into this distinction between 'spirits' and 'soul'? Which is she?

Tanous: Well, I feel that that was a spirit, and not a soul. The personality visiting and not the individuality. Perhaps the best way to put that particular case, is that it was like a bilocation. A bilocation is a person being in two places at once.

I think that I do make a distinction between an 'apparition' and a 'ghost'. A ghost, I feel, is a replay of the incident that happened, or someone seeing someone moving, yet there's really no dialogue. You know, one is seeing a brutal murder, who killed him, or a burning house. At least at this point, that's liable to change.

While an apparition is really a confrontation with a person, and you're talking to the person in the apparition. Now the person may look healthy and well from the time when he or she lived, like my confrontation with Isaac Newton in the Bermuda Triangle. He gave me proof, by taking my hand and drawing a zero-minus formula for me which was advanced calculus – there was no way for me to know. The confrontation was real.

And that is part of that Alex 2 experiment. Because when people see Alex 2, he is real like I am here, you can't tell the difference. They have often called me a living ghost. In other words, I should not be there, and yet I am there. Which would be a bilocation. Now, in an apparition, if a personality is here, and his individuality,

there is certainly a manifestation. So you see how closely it works with the Alex 2 experiment.

Interviewer: So a ghost then is more like something
left over, like leftover energy?

Tanous: I wouldn't call it leftover energy. I would call it
a historical incident, that has taken place, or a yearning
at the moment when someone dies, like that woman
who when she died, all her children were given to different people, adopted, and she wanted to visit to see
them, and she gave me at that time some hymns, or
parts of hymns, that the children recognized, to verify
that it was her.

Interviewer: I don't know that story.

Tanous: That's the black ghost one. She gave me certain
things to verify. While with the one in Maine, there
was no real verification that we could get, except the
footsteps, suggesting that the ghost was really there.

There always is a change when I interpret the information correctly. There have been times when the information was... there might have been several ghosts
in a house, and I picked one of them, but perhaps not
the one that may have been disturbing the house.

This building we're in now has many ghosts in it.
I've had meetings with them.

Interviewer: Apparitions or ghosts?

Tanous: They were apparitions. Like in the library: I was looking for a book one night when the door slammed and a little man appeared to me and gave me a message, speaking to me. I deliver the message and later found out who he was.

Interviewer: What was the message?

Tanous: Well the message was to Dr Osis. "Tell Dr Osis that I am pleased with what he is doing, and he will know who I am because at times I call him Karlis and at times I call him Osis." And we find out that it was a board member, the only board member in a picture who had died, who had been a close friend of Dr Osis.

Interviewer: What's the life of an apparition like? Where do they live?

Tanous: All they have learned is that they can regroup their molecules, and can appear and disappear, if they want to. Heaven is not up. It is a dimension… a state of mind. And they are closer than you are to me. And that's why they can have an influence on us. They can travel faster than the blinking of an eyelash.
At least these are my opinions and conceptions.

Interviewer: Do they have bodies?

Tanous: Yes. Which can materialize and dematerialize. They can go through walls and everything.

Interviewer: Is there one for every person?

Tanous: Yes. To me, we have two bodies. This physical one which we bury, and another body which is spiritual. By which I mean immaterial. Meaning it does not follow the law of nature – as we know it – but is more advanced in nature, and therefore can go through this table.

A good example is when I create Alex 2, he's already created. But when Alex 2 appears, he can go through a wall, he can be in Peru in a split-second, he can be anywhere in a split-second. Now let's reverse that. Let's say that Alex 2 creates Alex 1 in a scene, our sitting here, and let's say that we're all dead and so forth. You can then recreate sections of your life, and have it shown like a movie: there's talking, and telepathy, you know, your understanding and everything, it's the reverse.

Interviewer: Who can do that? You mean if you're a ghost you can do that?

Tanous: If you are an individual, the individuality of the person can do that. That's my opinion.

Interviewer: But then I could do that. But I can't...

Tanous: You can, but you haven't gone into it. Let's say that someone who is dead, or who has transcended, can recreate a scene that they once lived in for you. We're doing that with motion pictures. That's the best analogy. Or a negative. It's a negative.

∼

Tanous: I don't believe in devil possession. As an angel doesn't possess you, neither can a devil. A person who believes in devil possession... I believe that that's a personality problem.

Interviewer: Have you ever gone to a house – for ghosts – where people thought there was a possession?

Tanous: Yes. Some people had been told by others that they had a devil in the house, that it was possessed by evil, and all sorts of things. Certainly if you come from that religious point-of-view, you can create that. We went into a house where I was thrown out because I would not believe that someone was buried in the cellar. Because she believed that through some form, this information came to her – and I said, "Forget it."

Interviewer: Why didn't you believe it?

Tanous: Well, the woman was doing automatic writing. And the information came through the automatic writing. But I think automatic writing can be very un-conscious, 99 per cent is your unconscious, 1 per cent can be informational.

Interviewer: So she had you come to the house just to find this body in the basement?

Tanous: I said, "Forget it, there's no such person bur-ied anywhere." I can tell you that there had been an accident, where a young girl was brought into this house and died, and it turned out that the house had once been some kind of public place, before it be-came a house. But there was no one dead and bur-ied. And these are things that people get into. No more than people who say, for example, 'Person X is possessed by 36 demons'. I think that we have to be very realistic.

One of the realistic things that we must realize is that there has been certain manifestations which are leading us toward proof of life after death. But with 'demons' there is no proof. It's like people who've had near-death experiences and have been brought back; they seem to tell us the same story. Here we have cer-tain things that relate the same experience. You know, footsteps, apparitions, balls of light, and we have found this throughout all of history.

Interviewer: You mean ghost stories from the past?

Tanous: Of course, a lot of legend is attached to them, but there is a core of truth. I go back and see if they follow certain patterns.

We go into a location with a team. And we go through the house and tape my impressions. The occupants have already reported their manifestations (to others). And after the investigation is over, did I sense or see any of the same things that the inhabitants had seen in that house?

So, as we go through every room in the house, there it is: I report what I see, I don't know what the occupants originally saw. And then I make an evaluation. I meet ghosts everywhere. Everywhere I encounter some. But they may not all be having to deliver a message. They may just be very quiet ghosts.

You see, the experience that has occurred in a place, you and I sitting here, has now become a spirit. It's already recorded, so someone can walk in and say, "Here's Brad and Alex talking," and they see two people and they look like us and they're talking, alright. That is like a motion picture.

Interviewer: But why would it be played?

Tanous: If it needed to be played, it would be played. But if it didn't need to be played, it's still there. The camera has captured it. No more than your tape capturing it. When you replay this you're going to be replaying this experience.

Interviewer: What about actual film? Like the Amish people being afraid of having their snapshot taken because they're afraid it will take their soul. What does actual film do?

Tanous: Nothing at all. This is all legend. It's part of their belief. I respect it. But I'm a scientist as well as a psychic. And I've never seen it. No more than when they brought television into the Congo, and they took pictures and then showed the locals the pictures on their television. They were frightened seeing themselves because they couldn't understand what was taking place. No more than certain people say you have to release a possessed person with rituals and salt and benedictions, and things like this. I respect that, but I don't create certain things, which certain psychics do, like rituals and all manner of things, for their own ego-need. That's why the police and medical doctors and everyone else have to be extremely careful about whom they use to work with them.

Interviewer: What happens in a séance? Does that involve ghosts?

Tanous: I have never seen a séance with the holding of hands, the lightshow, and all this crap. I've never attended one. I believe that a ghost can appear in broad daylight, as they have appeared to me. I don't need candles, and table-lifting. That's all rigged. Rappings – I'm not saying that all of them are wrong. One night we were here, down-stairs, and I created a rapping which was heard on the table, but that was telekinetic, and the people said, "Oh yes. This is grandmother coming in." I said, "Come on. You don't even know what I was thinking about when I asked for the rap." And it was recorded.

There are very few people who can contact ghosts. A lot of them may *appear* to you, but making contact, getting information, and everything else, is different. A ghost can contact you. But not you contacting the ghost.

Interviewer: Can you do that?

Tanous: This is what I do. By going into the house and seeing what has taken place.

Interviewer: Well why 'you' – do you think?

Tanous: Why are you in your position and I in mine? Why was John Lennon shot? I don't know.

Interviewer: What about Ouija boards?

Tanous: What all that means, again I don't know. In a group you can have a group consciousness. I know of one case in Maine where the family was playing on a Ouija board and it said they should go to a graveyard, which they did, and then find the grave. They came back and said, "Well, you passed over." Then they went back and took a photograph and something appeared on film. And they did a whole series of these: photographs of the person who was dead. So there was a contact there over the Ouija board and they were able to make what we call 'psychic photography'. And they were tested and found legitimate.

I also hear that a priest in Chicago, I think Chicago, through a Ouija board helped the police by contacting and getting messages.

I think the strongest case in Chicago was this woman – she was not a psychic – who, while she was in a trance or sleep, received messages about who had killed a woman in the hospital, and the information of where the jewellery was, and that was how they arrested the murderer.

No more than the guy who was 'no psychic whatsoever,' who had a series of dreams of the DC–10 crashing in Chicago. He called up and there it was, it had crashed as he had seen it.

I've taken slides in a Church in Nice (California) and I have the ghosts there. I visited there three times and took pictures and I got ghosts all three times.

Interviewer: What did they look like?

Tanous: One of them is like a solid thing, but just half in transparency. The other is an energy in a completely different form.

Interviewer: Have ghosts helped solves crimes?

Tanous: Yes, I'm able to relive their events like a movie, and speak to them.

(End of existing interview transcript.)

6

THE SEARCH AND
RESEARCH OF SURVIVAL

Note: *This final chapter brings together several of the issues discussed in previous chapters, and Dr Tanous discusses the case for survival of human consciousness beyond death. It has been edited slightly to avoid reiteration of Dr Tanous' views, opinions, and beliefs which have already been outlined and discussed in the previous chapters.*

The subject of my inquiry is one of the greatest and most important questions of today: "Is there life after death?" We can add to that question: "What could possibly be the meaning of survival?"

We have all been called upon at one time or another to experience the pain of bereavement. We all have had the utmost desire to know what has happened to loved ones or to friends. Our mind has tried to fathom what conditions they exist in after their departure. Moreover, we realize that we, too, must make that journey one day. It is inevitable.

Until the present era, survival remained on the margins of theological belief, as an act of faith or philosophical speculation. But the mind of modern man has placed the problem of survival into an entirely new dimension.

I will deal with the "Search and Research of Survival," that I undertook with Dr Karlis Osis of the American Society for Psychical Research, and I will also draw from my personal and spontaneous experiences.

Religious beliefs in survival

I would like to take a few moments to speak about three major beliefs in survival. The first is that of Buddhism. This belief is held in a survival, but not a personal one. The Buddhist believes that he is part of God. If they did any evil in this life, they would have to return to atone for this. In other words, being part of God, therefore, they must be perfect to return into God. If they were not perfect they would take on a new body to make restitution for their evil acts. This is known as reincarnation.

The second belief in survival is that of the Jewish race. In the time of Christ, Jewish belief was in a kind of shadowy existence after death, but not an extension. This they spoke of as Sheol, and it has little certitude of immortality.

The third belief is in survival and immortality. It is the Christian belief. This basic concept is Egyptian, and it is that man has a body and a soul. After death, the soul would one day return to the body and the person would resurrect glorious and perfect. This was adopted by the Christians as one of their basic dogmas which was taken from the teaching of Jesus Christ.

We conclude, therefore, with three kinds of survival:

1. The reincarnationist, who believe that they are part of God and must return to God in perfection.
2. The Jewish who believe they are held in a shadowy existence, but not in a state of immortality.
3. The Christians, who believe that each individual has an independent survival body and soul and will be raised, one day, in perfection.

It is not my purpose to prove survival by religious belief, but rather to point out that mankind, universally, did believe in some form of existence after this life.

We have had no proof to rely on, and throughout history, we have tried to understand what it means to survive and what it is that survives. In what kind of consciousness do we exist?

What survives?

The problem we are faced with is to find what survives. Is it soul or spirit, or both? There is no solid scientific evidence that either exists or survives. We have a self-evident principle that life exists. What is it? According to the most accepted historical belief of philosophers and theologians, the soul survives after this life. They called this the principle of life. Once the soul leaves the body, a person dies.

The word 'spirit' has many meanings. The context I am using is that of the seat of consciousness. I identify it as the principle of our creative powers. I accept that soul or psyche gives one one's individuality; and the spirit gives one personality. According to Christian belief, spirit can be reborn again in this lifetime, but not the soul.

For example: the spirit of love, the spirit of justice, etc., and even the spirit of a particular person may be reborn, as when we say: "He or she has the spirit of his grandfather."

Having set this before you, I will go into both the spontaneous experience and the scientific work I have done on survival, with Dr Osis. I believe that they are equally important.

Birth of Alex 2

There are several reasons why I became interested in the scientific investigation of survival. My first experience was the most traumatic. It happened at the age of five. My mother was carrying a kettle of boiling water. She accidently tripped and the boiling water splashed all over me. I was not burned by the water. My parents decided to take me to the family doctor, who examined me and found nothing wrong with me. He suggested that I get some rest and see how I would be the next day.

As I started climbing the stairs, I looked up. I saw myself at the top of the stairs, not clearly, but I knew it was me. I waved and the other self waved back to me. Our friendship grew, and lasted several years. As time went on, the other self became clearer and I saw it was my double. I adopted him as my imaginary playmate.

It was this experience which led me, in later years, to many out-of-body experiences. I had had an early out-of-body experience, unlike those others (I speak of this for the first time), in which I had seen myself and my double, all at the same time. It was a strange experience. This also had an everlasting effect on me. I was caught, in some way, in a triangle. I have never heard of anyone having this kind of experience.

Personal encounter with survival

At the age of 11, I had another traumatic experience. I had my 'tri-experience'. I had been rushed to the hospital for surgery. Suddenly, I found myself out-of-body. I saw my physical body on the table. I saw my double standing nearby, and both of us watched the doctors and nurses operating on me.

Then at once, all disappeared. I encountered a dark line which I went through. I found myself in a beautiful light. This light came toward me and began to fill me, and then all was clear before me. I saw people I knew and some I did not know. I looked at myself, and the light had created something upon me, like a robe. I was living a beautiful experience – powerful and peaceful. I remember nothing else. When I awoke, it was to the music of the Armistice Day Parade.

These experiences were the starting point in my search for my other self.

Through the years, I have had countless experiences taking place, but the challenge came when I was asked by Dr Osis – if I could do it at will.

Testing for Out-of-body

The testing began. My first test was the 'fly-in' experiment. I had done very well in this; so well that another psychic saw me bend over the target table like a jackknife. I had not known that someone had seen me until months later, when Dr Osis delivered a paper on it.

So my work began – scientific research on the soul.

Two experiments were designed for me to do. The first was the Optical Image device. This is a structure about 2'x2'x3', inside which is a rotating disc divided into four quadrants, each of a different colour. On one of these quadrants, a small picture will appear (e.g., an image of a king, etc.). Each time the switch is thrown, one out of five possible target images is randomly selected and becomes visible on the disc. The quadrant and its colour are also randomly selected. The equipment is designed so that no one, including the experimenters, knows the final combination of quadrant, colour, and image during the experiment. The only way to see the whole thing is by looking through the small window in front of the Optical Image device. After the session, the experimenter decodes the information from the automatic recording machine to find out what the targets were.

This experiment took lots of hard work, but one day, I found the criteria. I experienced myself, out-of-body, as a spot of consciousness. I felt like a light. First this light is large, and then it comes to a point like a needle. I had the sensation of an 'I am' feeling. My scoring patterns were consistent with the OBE hypothesis: that there is something that can leave the body – some consciousness which could be thought of as leaving the body at death. My score was significant.

This led them to the second experiment with the colour wheel. This device is based upon a different optical principle, to help distinguish between various modes of perception. It is a sort of enclosed roulette wheel about 14" in diameter. In this case, the target is a coloured image on a black background. The only way to see the target correctly is to look precisely through the small window on the top of the box. Once again, I achieved a significant score in the experiment.

A series of three (two with the Optical Image and one with the colour wheel) gives these results: the average score of the three tests calculated on the law of probability is one out of a hundred. In the third series, independently, the law of probability would be one out of a thousand.

It was during this time that Alex 2 returned. He emerged from the light – and there he was! It was a spontaneous experience, but he has stayed with me since. We tested once for his presence with photo-multipliers and, in one session, we had outstanding results.

In the meantime, Dr Osis was thinking of new improvements for the Alex 2 experiment.

The Strain-Gauge Experiment

I was asked to go out-of-body and localize myself in a shielded chamber containing strain-gauge sensors placed in front of a viewing window of the Optical Image device. I was to identify randomly selected targets displayed in the Optical Image device. Unintentional mechanical effects on the strain-gauge sensors were registered on a Beckman polygraph during the time I was trying to identify the targets. When I was looking at the target, the strain-gauge activity level was significantly higher for trials which were hits than for trials which were misses. In all, 197 trials taken, of which 114 were hits and 83 were misses.

These results are interpreted as conforming to the hypothesis of the OBE experience; which is that the OBE consciousness, or a major part of the human personality, is externalized and exists apart from the physical body.

I was never told what was being tested in this experiment. As they continued testing, I remained unaware of what they were seeking. I preferred it that way.

What the current research on OBEs shows

1. When I project to another place, we find that my brainwave amplitudes seem to become modified, indicating electrical quiescence in the region of the brain at the back of the head

2. When out-of-body, my vision appears to be sharply localized at the spot where I say that

I am. Moreover, the lack of eye movement in the physical body during an OBE suggests that it is not merely a waking dream

3. It was found that there is a kinetic effect at the ostensible location of the OBE projection during perceptual testing
4. My giving the correct description of pictures would indicate that something of me has actually been out of the box, while an inaccurate description would reveal my absence.

The major results of the analysis showed that the sensory plates were significantly more active at the times when I was scoring a hit on the visual target than at the times I scored a miss.

This not only suggests that there is a physical effect at the location to which I project, but that the OBE might be a fluctuating process. It seems that I might have projected more of myself, out-of-body, on a hit target, than I do at other times during misses.

Apparitions as proof of survival

While still working on the Optical Image device, we were doing work on apparitions as another source for the proof of survival. I will not go into what an apparition is, but will rather explain our work in the field.

Apparition reports are as frequent as UFO sightings. People from all walks of life have reported them. What are they? There are many theories on the subject, but we really do not know. I have been a channel of communication with other dimensions most of my life, and I have not come to any definite conclusion. I do feel that apparitions are some kind of consciousness which makes itself visible, and are more perfect than we are. In other words, the higher consciousness can make itself visible to the lower consciousness. This appears to be seen in Christian lives of saints, angels, and holy people who have transcended.

My work is to make contact with this entity or consciousness and see what kind of problem they are burdened with, and to help release them.

In one case, I was taken to a Quaker church which was erected in the 18th century. It is now rented by another denomination. I was only told that there were some disturbances taking place.

I entered the small church with Dr Osis and Donna McCormick, and walked to the front. There, before me, I saw people sitting in a court fashion. I saw a woman, dressed in white, with her husband. I saw another woman who was accusing the man of adultery. He and his wife said it was false, but the court found them guilty and banished them.

This seemed almost like a fantasy. No one knew if this had happened.

Dr Osis called the Quaker archives where the records were kept. The man there said, "Oh yes, that is right. I read the case." So here we found out that what I had said was true.

We worked on a number of cases and the research is being done on them. Will they help us to answer the question: "Is there life after death?" I believe it will.

The work was going on and it excited me. We had many unsolved questions:

1. What is it that I am talking to or seeing?
2. How can science prove it?
3. Is it clairvoyance?
4. Or, am I really talking to an entity?

More work must be done. I see myself as a pioneer. I am testing, exploring, and discovering through my ability. I believe this will give science an insight on what happens after death. I feel we are approaching scientific proof that there is an existence separate from this one. Our next step is to capture Alex 2 on film. These are just some of the contributions, on my part, to the search and research for the proof of ghosts and survival.

LOYD AUERBACH INTERVIEWS DR ALEX TANOUS

As mentioned in the introduction, in total, Dr Tanous spent around twenty years in association with the ASPR, working on various issues of psychical research, but primarily on out-of-body experiences and hauntings. During that time, parapsychologist Loyd Auerbach (later, faculty member at Atlantic University, Virginia Beach) was also spending time working with the ASPR. A news report was even carried out for TV which involved Dr Tanous, Dr Osis, and Loyd all being filmed regarding their research.

Loyd had many conversations with Dr Tanous over the years, and even had the opportunity to interview him in regard to his experiences with ghosts and hauntings, which appeared in Loyd's book – ESP, Hauntings and Poltergeists (1986). With Loyd's kind permission, the same interview is provided here:

Loyd Auerbach: In dealing with the people and the actual situations, especially in the case of apparitional situations, I understand you might do some actual intervention. How do you go about judging what's going on, and what do you do about it, especially if there's a 'ghost' there?

Alex Tanous: In the investigations that we do, I know nothing about the house when we first go in. I know what the questions are that I can ask, which Dr Osis will allow to be answered, [while maintaining] a scientific situation. First, how old is the house? Secondly, are there children in the house? And thirdly, are there problems among the people in the house? Also, are there any antiques in the house?

All these, to me, have an important factor, and I have deduced these over the more than ten years that I've been working on apparitions. The reasons that I have made these categories is that I've run across cases in which these entered into specific relationships as to why the apparition was there.

Let's take the first one of how old the house is. When there is a house that's very old, there are multiple consciousnesses, and the question is, why is it a certain family, or two or three, will have disturbances, where there might have been twenty people living in the house when there have been no disturbances. I have found it is related to the persons themselves living in the house. Something had happened to these people that is related to the ghost or the apparition, and the apparition is about to manifest itself.

Secondly, if there are children; I've found that children can have very uncanny ways of arousing apparitions. Many times, as I said in my book *Is Your Child Psychic?*, they become their playmates. I listen to what the children have to say.

I do believe that apparitions or ghosts or energy travel, and don't have to be in just one house. Therefore, I've found here that if there are antiques, the antiques may have effects on the house for many different reasons. When you look at these, you have to examine them from every area.

I also found many times that there are what I call 'visiting ghosts' that do not belong to the house. These are ghosts that are of promises made to the apparitions, that have not been fulfilled. In my book, *Beyond Coincidence*, you'll find one of the cases that I did in Brooklyn. They were Jewish people who were supposed to call their children after their great-grandfather and grandmother. They only named one child as promised, and there was a visiting ghost involved, due to the unfilled promise.

LA: When you talk about apparitions, do you differentiate between entities and 'recordings,' as in a haunting?

AT: It depends on what kind of apparition cases I have. In some they are like movies, which is an energy left there, and I relive the whole 'movie' of what happened, why they are there. Then there is an actual apparition which I talk to, and with which I have a dialogue. Those are very interesting because it's there that many messages come through of why certain things have happened. In other words, it goes beyond the energy or 'motion picture' aspect of it. By the way, I have never found an evil apparition. There are no evil apparitions. The only evil that exists is when the person who sees the apparition does not understand and becomes fearful and therefore attributes evil to the apparition. I have never been harmed by an apparition. And I have met, over the last ten years, about 1,500 apparitions.

LA: So you've never met a ghost you didn't like?

AT: I never met a ghost I didn't like, right.

LA: When you talk to them, I take it that it's not only to question them, but also to seek resolution for them, getting them to 'pass on,' as some put it.

AT: In a recent case I did, there had been a double death which had taken place at two different times. A promise had been made on the deathbed, by the husband to his wife, that he would wait for her. When she died, she kept coming back but seeing him in the same time-frame as when they had lived, whereas he had died in a different time-frame. So here was a case where I had to make a transition for them.

It must be understood that I make a clear distinction theologically and philosophically. The transitions that I make for them are not the transitions of the afterlife, they are the transitions of the unfinished business here on Earth. There's a big difference.

LA: So you don't actually give them the ticket, you just make sure they have the change for the ride.

AT: Yes, the Earthly change. The ticket to wherever they are is already there. It's the unfinished business on the planet Earth that needs to be done. What I do with them is fulfil or finish the unfinished business.

LA: Some psychics have said that often these apparitions are of spirits who supposedly don't realize they're dead.

AT: Well, yes, but what one is talking about there is the human element, not the spiritual element. On the spiritual level they certainly know they have transcended and where they are. No one has made that distinction before.

LA: A spiritual versus a human element of apparition?

AT: Right.

LA: What about situations where it seems that communication is actually going across time, from the present back to the physical time the person, the apparition, was living in?

AT: When I talk about the motion-picture aspect, that's certainly an aspect of the past that's still going on. They always will be, because energy is always there. It's like a movie that's going to go on. What we've done is entered into their time and space. Apparently most of the ones like that welcome me into their time in space.

LA: Have you ever haunted anyone?

AT: Yes, in the sense of apparitions of the living, because I've appeared all over and records have been made of that.

THE TRUTH BEHIND AMITYVILLE

The Amityville house famously became immortalised for its alleged haunting reputation back in 1979. This was caused by the book *The Amityville Horror: A True Story*, by Jay Anson (1977), and the hit motion picture *The Amityville Horror*, directed by Stuart Rosenberg (1979). But the truth of the matter often becomes lost in the rumours and media presentations surrounding the case. There are many people today who are convinced that the building housed supernatural activity, while others believe this was brought on by various unspeakable crimes that took place within the building's history.

Of the many cases of paranormal phenomena that get picked up by the media, it is likely that Amityville was subject to the most lies and inaccuracies. The story of Amityville focuses on the Lutz family, and parapsychologists such as the late Prof Robert Morris noticed when reviewing the book (for *The Skeptical Inquirer*) that there were numerous inaccuracies regarding information about times, dates, the family, and investigative organisations mentioned within the book. This could be due to Jay Anson never having visited the house during the writing of the book, or the first clue that *honesty* was never going to be a strong feature of the Amityville case.

Few have had official requests or permission to investigate the property through scientific organizations and university departments. And yet there are many who claim that they did investigate the house with noted parapsychologists – when in fact they hadn't. However, through the ASPR, Drs Alex Tanous and Karlis Osis spent sometime within the Amityville house, and conducted an official preliminary investigation for the ASPR files.

Much like some of the information within this book, the information surrounding the Amityville investigation can be found in several sources. But it has been brought together here to present a clearer picture of the events specifically regarding Dr Tanous' involvement. Loyd Auerbach presented an honest and thorough discussion of the details of the investigations in his book *ESP, Hauntings and Poltergeists* (1986). Additionally, several letters regarding Amityville written by Dr Tanous have been archived by the Alex Tanous Foundation for Scientific Research.

The first investigation with genuine paranormal researchers, or more so, parapsychologists, involved Dr Osis of the ASPR, and Dr Jerry Solfvin, who at the time was associated with the Psychical Research Foundation, North Carolina. (Other sources discuss visits to the house by author Hans Holzer, and 'demonologists' Ed and Lorraine Warren, who spent a considerable amount of time in the house. But we need not discuss those separate events here which weren't specifically related to Dr Tanous' investigation).

In a discussion with Loyd Auerbach on the Amityville case, Dr Solfvin said that in early 1976 he received a call from the Lutz family, around 12th or 13th January. George Lutz explained the situation with the house to Dr Solfvin. At the time, Dr William Roll was away from the Psychical Research Foundation, so it was arranged for Dr Keith Harary and Dr Solfvin to have regular phone calls with George Lutz over the next several days to give updates on the haunting activity at Amityville. But in Dr Solfvin's opinion, it just didn't seem interesting enough (or perhaps credible enough) to warrant a trip over to investigate the matter.

Dr Solfvin discovered via a colleague of Dr Harary – who visited the house at the time due to living close to the place – that a priest had visited the family on several occasions during the alleged haunting. In Dr Solfvin's opinion, nearly everything described by the family was subjective, there was nothing to follow up of any interest, and therefore false perception or fraud seemed to be the answer.

A few months later, Dr Solfvin was in the New England area and stopped by New York. He called the Lutzes to tell them that he was in town, and that he'd like to speak with them in person. By this time the family had moved and were living just a few miles away. However, by pure coincidence (perhaps?), this was the exact same afternoon that Drs Tanous and Osis went to investigate the house. They visited the house first, and then stayed with the family for a while to interview them and ask questions. After the meeting was over, this gave Dr Solfvin a chance to speak to Dr Tanous privately about the matter.

Though the conversation was not officially documented, from Dr Solfvin's memory – relating the event to Loyd Auerbach – Dr Tanous asked Dr Solfvin what he thought of the place, as he saw nothing physically, and felt nothing psychically in the house, adding: "I think this is a real hoax." During the investigation and while interviewing the Lutzes, Dr Tanous caught more than a glimpse of a contract outlining the rights and gains of both the book and film promoting the alleged Amityville 'haunting'. This was all the investigators needed to assure themselves that their time was being wasted, and that the case should be left there and then. Dr Solfvin went over to the house to check this out for himself, but by the time he got there, the Warrens had already turned up with film crews and journalists. Luckily, Drs Tanous and Osis had managed to avoid this – just!

Amityville had been a media money-making machine, and was potentially dangerous to any serious researcher having their name attached to it. Especially if such a researcher were to have publicly claimed there might have been something paranormal going on, thus fuelling the media cash-cow, and tainting the public's view – as well as the credibility – of parapsychology and paranormal research.

Both Drs Tanous and Osis were glad to have left the situation as soon as possible. In further private conversations with Loyd Auerbach, Dr Tanous said that he never felt anything in the house, nor did he experience anything that was claimed to have regularly occurred in the house in terms of paranormal activity. Dr Tanous also said that he was quoted in some article as having said that he had "seen the devil" in the house, which needless to say, he argued as untrue.

Such outrageous and obscure quotes were a regular occurrence with the media mayhem of Amityville, as Dr Tanous was quoted as having said and done several things inside the house, which in fact he hadn't. Some people even wrote to him, to inform him about such quotes being made on TV and radio. Below is Dr Tanous' response to one such letter that was sent to him:

Dear Barbara,

Thank you for your letter of October 2, 1979, in regards to the statement made by Ed Warren on the Brian Dow Radio Show on September 1, 1979, that I had levitated two feet off the ground in the Amityville House, which is <u>untrue</u>. I personally found nothing that resembled any of the paranormal things mentioned in the book.

An article which appeared in the *Star* after my visit said that I had said that it was demonic forces at work, which is also <u>UNTRUE</u>. Anyone who knows me, knows that I DO NOT BELIEVE IN DEVIL POSSESSION.

In regards to the contract, etc., I cannot make any statement on this since all my findings are property of the American Society for Psychical Research. What was said in private conversation to Steven Kaplan was not meant to be, nor can it be, published since it would break my contract with the ASPR.

Should Dr. Karlis Osis wish to clear the information and that it is released by him what happened, then it would be OK with me. The only thing the ASPR has said, quoted from *Newsday*, November 17, 1977, is that we bowed out because of "the commercial overtones."

My congratulations on the research you are doing on the house. I feel that the people should know the truth.

If I can be of any further assistance to you, do not hesitate to write.

YOURS TRULY
ALEX

CC: Dr K Osis.

This letter emphasizes that Amityville was realised to be a fraudulent case. And, even with the slightest chance of it ever having had paranormal occurrences at any time, the chances of any suitable investigations being conducted, at that time, had been tarnished by the media frenzy. Following on from this, Dr Tanous knew his reputation, and that of the ASPR, was on the line if they became officially involved in the case when they knew so much false information was being created and passed around. Therefore, he wrote to the relevant TV and radio companies to have them either retract false statements and information, or at least clarify the truth:

Dear Sir:

On September 1st a.m., on the Brian Dow show, called "True Inside Story of Amityville," with George

Lutz, the Warrens, Rick Moran, and Steve Kaplan, I understand it was stated – and later reported to me that this was stated, by Steve Kaplan – that Mr. Ed Warren made the statement that I had levitated two feet off the ground when I was doing the research at the Amityville house.

I would like to verify if this statement was indeed made, for, if it was, I want you and your listeners to know that this statement that I levitated two feet is untrue. Furthermore, in my investigation, I witnessed nothing paranormal existing in the house.

I would appreciate hearing from you regarding a clarification of this statement.

Thank you for your assistance.

YOURS TRULY
ALEX TANOUS

Loyd Auerbach also took the opportunity to ask Dr Osis if they thought the whole case was a hoax before the investigation, and especially before Dr Tanous discovered the contract. To which, Dr Osis' reply was: "I think before, I simply wanted to know more... Alex, in the house, did not see anything to the Lutzes story at all. Right there, he took a negative stand to it. He didn't see anything to the phenomena which were reported by the Lutzes. I still wanted to go through with the interview. I just did the best I could, and good luck brought us the clinching thing, the contract. I think we got good insight into it, but the real exposés were the journalists' work. There were two of them, who called from *Newsday*. There was also a local Amityville paper which called up and published quite a reasonable article" (Auerbach, 1986, pp. 301-302).

Drs Tanous and Osis missed, or more so, narrowly avoided the wave of media frenzy at Amityville which followed, particularly with regards to the Warrens involvement. Even so, respectable research organisations such as the ASPR were still hassled by the media, and claims that parapsychologists had fully investigated the house and either 'found it credible' or had 'a strange experience in the house' were still made. It was an unavoidable media vortex at the time, though I think it is fair to say that not everyone saw it coming. Each case of a haunting does need to be judged on its merits and cannot be generalised to the rest. Amityville was at least given a chance by the ASPR and the Psychical Research Foundation. However, it seems that the *true* investigators quickly discovered it for what it was, especially Dr Tanous.

APPENDIX 3

JENNIFER ALLEN'S MEMORIES

The following section was kindly written by Jennifer Allen for the purpose of this book. Here we have a brief insight into the unusual events surrounding her meeting Dr Tanous for the first time, experiences that people tended to have on their trips to Egypt with Dr Tanous (of which he undertook several, combining mysticism and spirituality with the history and enigmas of Egpyt's hidden past and present landmarks), and finally, a first-hand account of Alex's personal visits to alleged haunted locations he was invited to (in this case, by a close friend).

Jennifer was a great friend of Dr Tanous for around twenty years and up till the point of his death. Even *beyond this, Jennifer still shares in his teachings and has presented on his life and work at the Rhine Research Center (Durham, USA) in recent years. This also gave Jennifer the chance to share her own personal experiences with Dr Tanous as well as the wealth of interests he was known to have that are not all on paper or published in books or journals. Some of the most interesting aspects of Dr Tanous and the projects he was involved in are now in many cases part of memories alone.*

When personal memories are written down and shared (as below), they can sometimes tell us so much more about what we know in the present about history, peoples' experiences, changes over time, thereby allowing further insight into what certain individuals who are no longer with us were like. We can only achieve this if we are given the precious chance to look to the past.

Alex Tanous – Ghostbuster, Healer, Teacher, Friend

Strange Beginnings

Flashing back to an afternoon in 1976, I was 29 years old, a mother of an 18-month-old daughter, co-owner of a bookstore, and treasurer of my church. I stopped by the rectory to talk with our minister about church affairs and sitting in his living room was Alex Tanous. Even though I had not read his autobiography yet, I recognised Alex since I had a stack of his new book,

Beyond Coincidence, selling rapidly in my bookstore. The minister explained Alex had been asked by our local police to help them find two missing girls who had each run away for different reasons. Alex asked me to stay and said he would show the minister and me how the universe provides signs or clues showing how a person had disappeared. He held a piece of one girl's clothing and started thinking of the girl. He stated that she had been picked up at the local park and driven away in a red car, and then told us to look outside to watch the cars passing the church. Practically every vehicle that drove by was red! He said she was in danger from the people she ran away with, asking the minister to not tell the parents about the danger; and then he concentrated, sending her energy to call her parents within 24 hours.

Alex told me later that she had called home by the next day and told her parents that the people she was with were trying to force her to take acid and other drugs. They paid for a bus ticket to bring her home. Alex reported that he thought the second girl had died, and he asked us to not go to the parents with negative information. Alex did not like telling people about negative results or futures. We talked all afternoon about spirituality and parapsychology. Then when I left the rectory, I went to my store and picked up his book, reading it all night until I finished it.

Since I had read about Alex's many healings, the next day I called the minister and asked if he had a phone number for Alex because I knew a young man who was in the local hospital suffering from pains throughout his body, yet the doctors could not figure out what he had. The minister told me that Alex had left his unlisted number stating that, "She is going to need to talk with me so please give Jennifer my phone number when she asks." We talked for hours that day, starting a friendship that would last for over twenty years, enveloping my four daughters, of whom he became a Godfather to each one. (My parents became so close to Alex that they travelled to Egypt with him in 1983.) Alex told me to tell the boy's mother that her son had been poisoned by arsenic that may have been given to him in a drink. He said that she needed to take him to Dartmouth Hitchcock Hospital where the doctors are trained to detect poisoning. It turns out that he played drums in a local band and had been sick since his last gig. The mother did not want to tell the Portsmouth doctors what they should do so he unfortunately suffered for another week, until she finally broke down and asked them to check for arsenic poisoning. Low and behold, Alex was correct, and after the boy was taken up to Dartmouth Hitchcock Hospital to meet with specialists, he had his blood cleaned out through long periods of Chelation therapy; he was cured of all of his aches and pains.

Alex asked my minister and me to attend many semesters of his classes in Portland, ME. Over the next 15 years, we took almost every class he taught. The students were taught to see auras, how to open up to heal others, and how to pass many parapsychological tests, as taught at The Rhine Research Center, the Institute for Parapsychology at Duke, and at the American Society of Psychical Research (ASPR) in New York City. Alex had been gifted from early on to be able to see if people were healthy, ill, or going to die, and even to detect where and what the illness was. He wanted everyone he met to realize that everyone could be healers and could astro-travel (like Alex 2) if they would just open up their minds and allow God's energy to flow through. I was able to experience this in a remarkable way that was proven to be true in the story below.

Dr Elisabeth Kübler-Ross & experiences in Egypt

In 1981, I introduced Alex to Elisabeth Kübler-Ross (EKR), whom I had met due to my involvement with Hospice and from attending her Life, Death, & Transition workshop in September 1981, and then her Spirituality workshop in October of the same year. I gifted EKR the book *Beyond Coincidence*. After reading it, she had her secretary call me to tell me that she had a dream and wished to know when she could meet him. Due to both of their busy schedules, it took six months for us to get them together. We drove to New York State and attended a weekend workshop on 'Forgiveness' that was facilitated by Elisabeth and Tara Singh, using the *Course in Miracles.* At the end of the workshop, people asked Elisabeth and Alex to talk about their psychic experiences and journey. They talked about seeing each other, 'out-of-body', at a gathering of well-known people that each had received an invitation to attend – a conference on Monday 12 October, 1981, in the Queen's Chamber at the Great Pyramid of Cheops at Giza, Egypt. Both Alex and Elisabeth had received hand-delivered invitations. They explained what had happened to each of them, including seeing President Anwar Sadat, who had been murdered weeks before. Elisabeth had met Sadat in person earlier in the year, when his daughter had asked Elisabeth to fly to Egypt to meet with her parents. After Elisabeth and Alex told their amazing stories, Alex turned to me and said: "Jennifer, I want you to tell them what happened to you."

The weekend of the out-of-body trip to Egypt, Elisabeth had told the story of her mysterious invitation to all who were gathered at her workshop on Spirituality in Connecticut (one of only two that she ever gave on this subject). She said she had lost her hand-delivered invitation but would be joining the group of 200 invitees as she flew to her next venue in Canada on Sunday afternoon at 2 p.m.

I will now include excerpts from a very personal letter I wrote to Elisabeth. She responded that she would go into detail at a later date with Alex and me, then affirmed that she had seen Anwar Sadat as I had witnessed below:

Dear Elisabeth,

... around 2:40 pm on Monday I left my body and joined you on the plane. We talked a lot about what I had been thinking about World Ecumenicalism ... you then said: 'Come on, Ginger (a nickname my mother gave me at birth), you're going to Egypt with me.' I knew I was supposed to take the place of one person who had decided to not go join the group of 200. We flew across the ocean, across Europe & down to Egypt and the pyramids. All sorts of powerful people were waiting. And Sadat was there, too. He came up to you and took your hand and welcomed you, and then you introduced me to him... I saw Alex Tanous fly in and hug me and say he had come, too!

Then we all walked down a red carpet into the pyramid. You took my left hand and Ram Dass took my right. (I had never met him or read his books at the time). The carpets became white, blue, and then in the Queens Chamber, the floor was a glittering gold and the room and pyramid pulsated with energy! I saw crystal diamonds, rubies, and sapphires hanging and glistening all over. A 'white glowing ball' appeared above the center and under it were all the signs of all the religions that are and ever were...

Ironically, when I returned to Rye, New Hampshire, that night, I had invited my friend Betty Hill to dinner with my family, and Alex drove from Maine to join us. He knew Betty from a Psychic Cruise they had been featured on together years earlier. Betty and I became friends through similar interests in UFOs, volunteering in our hometown of Portsmouth, New Hampshire, and social work. When I asked Alex if he had been in Egypt that afternoon, praying for world peace, he asked me how I knew. I then reported what I had seen. He stated that I must have been there and told me that he would give a copy of his invitation to me and one to Elisabeth. I also met Ram Dass years later in Cambridge, MA, and asked if he had been there. He acknowledged 'Yes' and said I definitely must have been with him there. During a stay in California in 1985, friends of mine introduced me to Timothy Wyllie and his partner. They were the ones who had created and sent out the invitation to celebrities and spiritual leaders all over the world. They gave me an original invitation that I still have today.

Ghostly experiences with Alex

In 1982, when we bought our 1903, four-storey, four-bedroom Victorian home in Portsmouth, New Hampshire, my husband at the time decided to build an art studio in our attic. He would come and tell me about strange sounds in the house, feet walking up the stairs, doors slamming shut, creaking noises, all with no one there. The Call family had built and lived in the house, including Mr Call's two spinster daughters who moved to a nursing home at an old age. Then, a young couple had moved in and stayed for two years, until they were transferred away by business. Since we had two daughters and one more on the way, we decided to put cement over our dirt floor basement, so we could add two more bedrooms to the house for guests. Once we had moved in, and after my mother kept having experiences where she would feel a cold energy brush by her arms and then she would find money on the floor, I asked Alex to come visit our new home.

The minute he arrived he felt a cold energy brush by his arm. He told me that the man who had built the house, Mr Call, was telling him that he had hidden money downstairs in the basement. He told me that Mr Call liked us and liked what we had done to his home. Unfortunately, we had covered the floor with cement, so I was never able to dig up a treasure. After Alex's visit, we did not feel cold energy or hear doors slamming anymore. Alex had assured Mr Call that we would take good care of his home. For years afterwards, even when we moved to California for a two-year stint, we kept finding money on our floor wherever we lived. We believed that Mr Call had travelled with us to California.

The same day Alex came to see us, I took him to visit my friend, who owned an old home on the ocean in Little Bay Harbor. He told her that he could see and feel many people in her over 200-year-old house. He stated that he saw a lady who once used to live there sitting upstairs in one of her rooms. She was a friendly ghost. To this day, my friend tells me she was afraid to hear about the ghosts, so she would not discuss it with anyone and wanted to forget that Alex had seen people in her home. Alex could detect energies and ghosts whenever he walked into a home that was affected by spirits. He would talk with them and help them go to the light to find peace whenever he could.

Alex was always willing to travel any distance to help people solve problems with ghosts, missing relatives, or sickness. He never took money for this. Sometimes, the police would insist on giving him gas money or a meal. I watched him turn down every single offering from those who offered him money for healings or psychic experiences. Alex told me that he made his money from his teaching, and that what he did was a God-given gift that he was simply a vessel for. Alex was a loving, healing, light-bearing brother who still works through those who knew him to send healing energies to those in need.

Jennifer R. Allen
August 14, 2013

APPENDIX 4

ALEX TANOUS –
GHOSTBUSTER

As was briefly mentioned in the introduction, Dr Tanous contributed many interviews to newspapers, locally as well as internationally. Many of the local newspaper pieces of the 1980s mention that the writers/journalists were given the opportunity to spend time with Dr Tanous in his daily life, either during his lectures at the University of Southern Maine or by attending a ghost-hunt with him. One particular writer who became interested in his work was Thomas Verde, who not only wrote an article on Dr Tanous entitled "Alex Tanous, Ghostbuster" for Casco Bay Weekly (Verde, 1988), but also wrote his own book on the local hauntings of Maine (Verde, 1995).

The following section is a summarised and edited version of Mr Verde's article discussing the ghost-hunting exploits of Dr Tanous with Mr Verde. This adds additional insight into his work and opinion on ghosts and hauntings.

The McClellan–Sweat House

The McClellan–Sweat house took on the persona of the stereotypical haunted house portrayed in films. At the time of the Tanous/Verde investigation, white dust sheets covered the furniture, hooks were still fixed on the walls where paintings once hung, the staircase squeaked, and there was an echo in every room of the house.

Mr Verde noted that Dr Tanous needed only himself to carry out an investigation of the property (unlike Dr Osis who used various pieces of environmental monitoring equipment). Trusting in his own abilities was all Dr Tanous required to either obtain information about the building or its history, or to communicate with the dead. The two gentlemen were also joined by Sarah Cecil, the Portland Museum of Art's public information assistant. The house was connected to the Museum as it had been built by Mrs Sweat in 1911, in memory of her late husband.

Within minutes of entering the building, it appeared that contact had been made with the spirits. While they stood at the bottom of the grand staircase, a subtle chill in the air was felt by everyone, which appeared to be drifting down the staircase.

"I hear music," said Dr Tanous. "There's some kind of music being played here, like a party or a celebration. It sounds like a spinet" (a spinet being a 16th-century harpsichord).

Upon turning to the history records, it was discovered that Mrs Sweat was famous for holding grand parties in her home, and it was likely that much of the activities had taken place where the trio were then standing.

"Is there a small room here somewhere?" asked Dr Tanous. "I'm looking for a small room." Ms Cecil guided them up to the third floor where Dr Tanous found what he was looking for – a large plaque that used to be on the building describing its history and how it had been bequeathed to the Portland Museum of Art. Part of the terms of Mrs Sweat's gift had been that the house should not be altered or changed in any way that would change the overall character of the 19th-century mansion.

Dr Tanous felt that the building had been left empty for too long, and whatever form of ethereal consciousness did reside in the building was eager for life to be brought back in the building (i.e., people, social gatherings, and parties were what the building and more so the dead required once more). In response to this, Mr Verde asked Dr Tanous if he thought the ghosts were 'lonely' now that the building had been vacated and left untouched.

"They could be," Dr Tanous said with a smile. "But this place has what we call 'historical energy'. In other words, there's a compilation of historical aspects here and in the house next door. This means it will always, 'always' be a historical corner, you'll never be able to destroy it. But I know that it will be restored, at least that's what I feel from the energy."

Ms Cecil explained that the Museum was still looking for money to assist with the restoration of the mansion. It was suggested that the building's haunting reputation was putting potential funders off the idea.

Alex Tanous – Ghostbuster

Being the 1980s and the decade in which the well-known motion picture *Ghostbusters* was released, Dr Tanous was rather amused by the term when he was referred to as a 'ghostbuster'.

"I like the term," he said. "I'm sorry I didn't think of it myself. But real ghostbusting doesn't mean that you send the ghost away; it merely means that you become friends with the ghost."

Mr Verde believed that if this statement was so, then Dr Tanous had a lot of 'friends'. Indeed, we could look at the notion of 'ghost-hunting' as becoming friends with the ghosts, or at least becoming acquainted with the areas in which they haunt. Any good investigator will spend several weeks, months, or even years in a haunted location in order to understand the exceptional experiences previously reported. Dr Tanous had worked at numerous haunted locations throughout Maine and beyond, including: a haunted mill in Oxford County inhabited by the ghost of an ex-worker; a home in Cape Elizabeth believing that the 19th-century owner was still there entertaining other ghostly friends; and Portland's West End where he was reported to have sensed the presence of several ghosts.

Ghostbusting in real life

In the early days of psychical research, Dr Tanous would have been referred to as a 'medium,' i.e., one who believes s/he has the ability to contact the dead. Things have moved on from experiments of the séance room, and now attempts to 'contact the dead' take place in the laboratory, with the help of psychologists, physicists, and the latest medical and environmental monitoring equipment.

Dr Tanous coined a term for a modern psychic – a 'psionic' – reflecting the marriage of the Greek roots for 'mind' (psyche) and 'ionic', which Dr Tanous said referred to the current technological aspects of the science.

Ghostbusting for Dr Tanous usually followed the same routine:

"I'm not told anything about the house, beyond the fact that there have been disturbances there," as he put it. "When I go in, I enter an altered state and then have a talk with the ghost through telepathy. I see them and they see me. Then everything I say is recorded or written down. Once that is done, we then have a conversation with the people who saw the ghost and we tell them what the ghost is doing there and why. Then we ask them whether they want the ghost to leave or not, and if they do we inform the ghost that there's no need to make themselves visible. They can still stay there, but it's just that the people aren't accustomed to having a ghost live with them. In one case, though, we had a woman who didn't want the ghost to leave because it was her mother. So, we just left her there."

Dr Tanous referred to what he did as 'ghost healing' or 'ghost psychiatry' because his work involved attempting to help each ghost understand where it is and what 'time zone' it is. In other words, offering reassurance to the dead – and the bereaved who witnessed the ghosts of the dead. Sometimes, Dr Tanous just listened to the problems that ghosts presented in order to determine why it may have been haunting a particular area.

In the relatively unclear world of psychic investigation, Dr Tanous made a clear distinction between ghosts and apparitions.

"An apparition," he said "is someone really present there. We speak of that in religion, for example, with the apparition of a saint appearing at such and such a place. This means that the person who has died is physically there and physically visible. All we know is that the person who has transcended has the ability to sway in and out of time. In other words, they can come back and make their case known to us."

The Maine Triangle

Dr Tanous believed that there is a lot of paranormal activity in Maine due to its geography. He had done research on the Bermuda Triangle and was closely involved in the making of a film on the area entitled *Mysteries Beyond the Triangle*. It was his theory that in apposition to the negative triangle formed by Florida, Bermuda, and Puerto Rico, there is a relatively positive one encompassing, roughly, Maine, its coast, and the Bay of Fundy. Running horizontally across the middle of the "Maine Triangle," said Dr Tanous, is a "belt of very strong activity." He further added, "the negative energy goes down," pointing to the Caribbean on a hastily sketched map, "the positive energy flows up." "Up" means us.

At least one other person involved in quasi-mystical research thought along the same lines as Dr Tanous regarding Maine's positive energy on the globe

– controversial scientist Dr Wilhelm Reich (who lived in Rangeley, Maine). During the 1950s, Dr Reich believed in something called 'orgone energy'. He said that science couldn't measure it because of inadequate equipment, but as close as we can tell, 'orgone energy' had something to do with sexual energy and cloud formations. Dr Reich, a native of Austria, chose Maine as his home because he felt that the state was the centre of a lot of orgone energy.

How to deal with a ghost

Dr Tanous was not in favour of just anyone going out to investigate claims of paranormal phenomena and hunt for ghosts in privates homes. He believed that "more harm than good" could come of such events if not carried out by the appropriate professionals. For example, Dr Osis and he held qualifications in psychology and counselling. Therefore, on one level, they were entirely capable of dealing with any psychological issues that haunted locations could potentially throw at them. In other words, should a percipient be under a lot of stress or be suffering from various side-effects of traumatic social events (a family death, relationship trouble, past abuse, etc.), the Tanous/Osis team were qualified to deal with such situations and handle them in an ethical, professional, and appropriate manner, with the percipient's health and well-being taking top priority.

People who believed that they had had strange experiences were urged by Dr Tanous to contact the American Society for Psychical Research (or the British branch). Offering reassurance that someone there would be willing to help and investigate the claims.

"All this is done very scientifically," said Dr Tanous, "and all our records are kept extremely confidential. Persons at the society will contact me and we send a ghostbusting team in or we may just handle it over the phone."

Today, this is still the case. Even though there is an increase in independent paranormal investigation groups (many of which are in it for the wrong reasons, i.e. thrill seeking), the Society for Psychical Research is still very much active – specifically the British branch. People who believe they have had haunting experiences, or are living with a poltergeist, are encouraged to make contact and have the issue dealt with in a discreet and professional manner by experienced researchers and scholars (and not just by avid fans of *Ghostbusters!*).

References

Verde, T. A. (1988). "Alex Tanous, Ghostbuster". *Casco Bay Weekly*, 27 October, 7–9.

Verde, T. A. (1995). *Maine Ghosts and Legends*. Camden, ME: Down East Books.

ABOUT THE AUTHORS

Alex Tanous, D.D. (1926–1990), came from Portland, Maine, and was an international teacher of philosophy, well-being, and parapsychology. He was the author of several books, including: *Beyond Coincidence, Is Your Child Psychic?*, and *Dreams, Symbols and Psychic Power.* He spent many years working with groups and families investigating psychic phenomena, including his own abilities, through the American Society for Psychical Research. He held five degrees, including a bachelor of arts in theology, three masters degrees in theology, philosophy, and education, and a doctorate in theology (doctorate in divinity). He guest-lectured all over the world, and regularly in the colleges and universities of New York. His most frequent lecturing post was at the University of Southern Maine, where he had given lectures on healing, dreams, and had established the first parapsychology course within the USA to be taught with credit.

Callum E. Cooper is a psychologist and a doctoral candidate based at the University of Northampton (UK), within the psychology division's *Centre for the Study of Anomalous Psychological Processes.* He is a member of the Society for Psychical Research, the Parapsychological Association, the Academy for Spiritual and Consciousness Studies, and a Hope Studies Graduate Researcher (Hope Studies Central, University of Alberta). His research and lecturing cover topics such as: parapsychology and anomalous experiences, the psychology of death & bereavement, positive psychology, and Egyptology (regarding ancient mysticism). He has lectured on parapsychology in the USA and throughout the UK. In 2009, he was award the Eileen J. Garrett Scholarship from the Parapsychology Foundation. He has received the Alex Tanous Scholarship Award from the Alex Tanous Foundation for Scientific Research, three times over, and has remained strongly associated with the Foundation ever since. Additionally, he is the author of *Telephone Calls from the Dead.*

INDEX

Paperbacks also available from White Crow Books

Leo Tolstoy with Simon Parke—
Conversations with Tolstoy
ISBN 978-1-907355-25-7

Howard Williams with an
Introduction by Leo Tolstoy—*The
Ethics of Diet: An Anthology
of Vegetarian Thought*
ISBN 978-1-907355-21-9

Vincent Van Gogh with
Simon Parke—*Conversations
with Van Gogh*
ISBN 978-1-907355-95-0

Wolfgang Amadeus Mozart
with Simon Parke—
Conversations with Mozart
ISBN 978-1-907661-38-9

Jesus of Nazareth with
Simon Parke—*Conversations
with Jesus of Nazareth*
ISBN 978-1-907661-41-9

Thomas à Kempis with Simon
Parke—*The Imitation of Christ*
ISBN 978-1-907661-58-7

Julian of Norwich with Simon
Parke—*Revelations of Divine Love*
ISBN 978-1-907661-88-4

Allan Kardec—*The Spirits Book*
ISBN 978-1-907355-98-1

Allan Kardec—*The
Book on Mediums*
ISBN 978-1-907661-75-4

Emanuel Swedenborg—
Heaven and Hell
ISBN 978-1-907661-55-6

P.D. Ouspensky—*Tertium
Organum: The Third
Canon of Thought*
ISBN 978-1-907661-47-1

Dwight Goddard—*A
Buddhist Bible*
ISBN 978-1-907661-44-0

Michael Tymn—*The
Afterlife Revealed*
ISBN 978-1-970661-90-7

Michael Tymn—
*Transcending the Titanic:
Beyond Death's Door*
ISBN 978-1-908733-02-3

Guy L. Playfair—*If This Be Magic*
ISBN 978-1-907661-84-6

Guy L. Playfair—*The Flying Cow*
ISBN 978-1-907661-94-5

Guy L. Playfair —*This
House is Haunted*
ISBN 978-1-907661-78-5

Carl Wickland, M.D.—
Thirty Years Among the Dead
ISBN 978-1-907661-72-3

John E. Mack—*Passport
to the Cosmos*
ISBN 978-1-907661-81-5

Peter & Elizabeth Fenwick—
The Truth in the Light
ISBN 978-1-908733-08-5

Erlendur Haraldsson—
Modern Miracles
ISBN 978-1-908733-25-2

Erlendur Haraldsson—
At the Hour of Death
ISBN 978-1-908733-27-6

Erlendur Haraldsson—
*The Departed Among
the Living*
ISBN 978-1-908733-29-0

Brian Inglis—*Science
and Parascience*
ISBN 978-1-908733-18-4

Brian Inglis—*Natural and
Supernatural: A History
of the Paranormal*
ISBN 978-1-908733-20-7

**All titles available as eBooks, and selected titles available in Hardback
and Audiobook formats from www.whitecrowbooks.com**